Esti Glazer - Painter

Published by: Yotzrim Art Gallery - Consulting and selling art
Design: Roni oz

© All rights reserved to Yotzrim Art Gallery - Consulting and Sale of Art- 2021
www.yotzrimgallery.com

Address: PO Box 5123, Herzliya, ZIP Code 4649719
Phone: +972-54-5286808

Do not reproduce, copy, photograph, record, translate, store in a database, transmit or receive in any way or transmit data from it in any form or electronic means, optical or mechanical or otherwise - any part of the material in this book. Commercial use of any kind of material contained in this book is strictly prohibited without the prior permission of the creators of the gallery.

Esti Glazer - Painter

The subjects of the paintings I create are urban and natural sceneries as an expression of my love to world I am surrounded by and my curiosity to know it and tour it. In my trips in our wonderful and loved country, of the sceneries. Looking at the photographs I took, and by their inspiration creates a painting rich in colors. In my paintings I express my feelings that are expressed in the color I use. I paint on canvas or paper glued to a wood.

My work is planned in advance and goes through several stages of work. I have developed two techniques with which I work and undergo a process of learning and improvement. One technique of creating several layers of paint on each other using a spleen that makes the work to show material, rich and volume. And the second is a technique of scratching the layers of fresh paint with a spade and creating layers of intense color. This technique corresponds with the children's work - the scratching of layers of color from which the magic emerges.

In most of my paintings I paint in color, but sometimes I choose to paint entirely monochromatic or have surprising touches of a single color. I maintain balance and symmetry in the composition by organizing the geometrical shapes on the page and building complementary connections between the various elements in the painting, and harmony and balance are also present in the paintings in which the parts of the work are not identical and create contrasts of color and shape.

In my early works I was looking for precision and systematic skills and I chose to use paintbrush in an oil paint technique. In time i experimented with other techniques. Following my experimentation phase i got that working with paint and experiencing it unleash my creativity and had me start working a putty knife and loads of paint.

My passion to art began during my art studies courses as an early childhood education college student. One can see that more than 30 years of teaching young people influenced the techniques I choose to use and the naive context of my artistic expression. What guided me as a teacher was the commitment to leave the future generation with love for the arts and the access to bring creativity to any area of their life as adults.

I started to create when I was an Education student at Levinsky College, one of my specialties was art. Throughout my years as a teacher at the Ministry of Education, art and creativity were an inseparable part of my kindergarten program. At the same time I continued to study art with the artist Einan Cohen and continued with the artist Meir Natif.

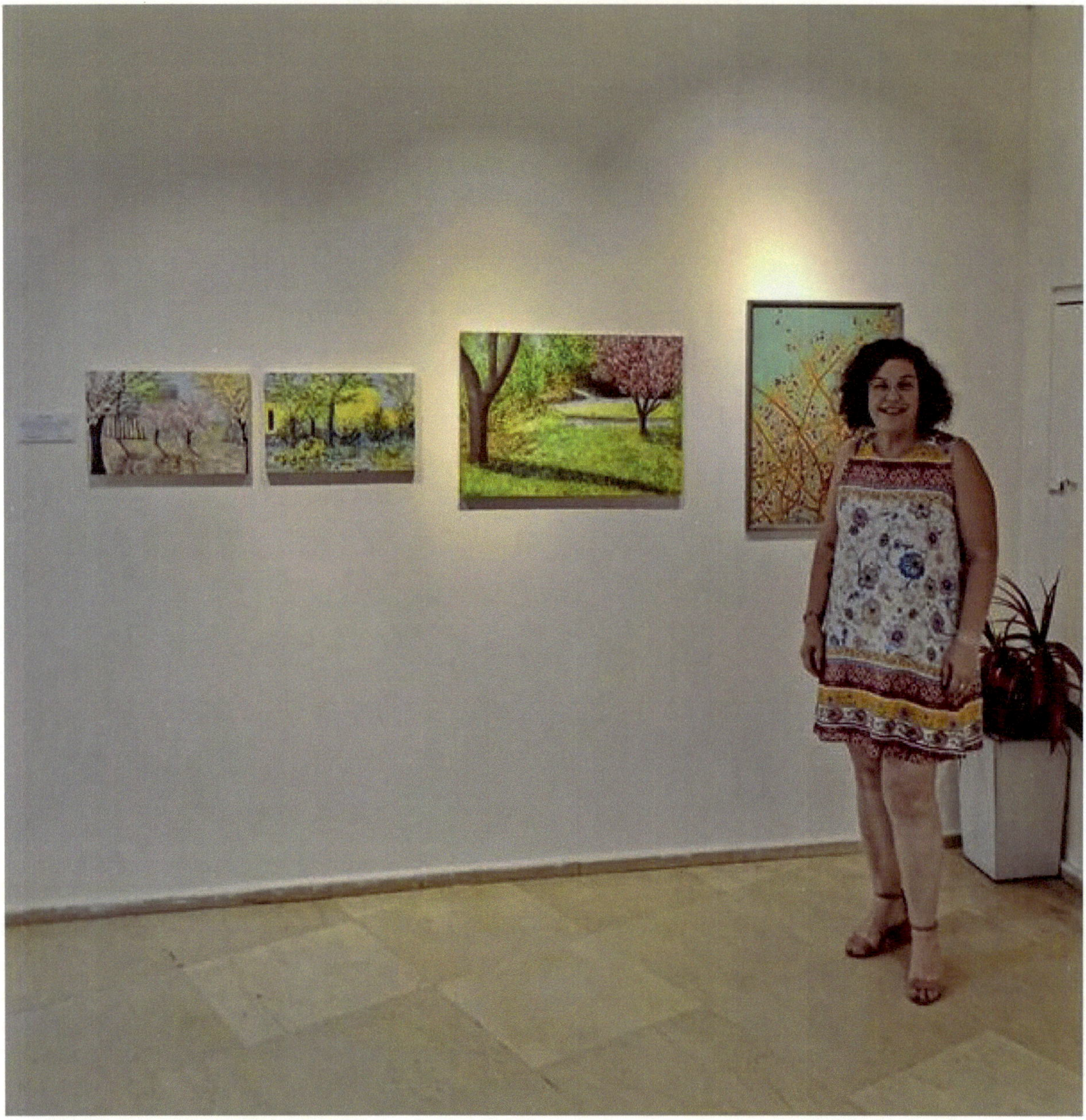

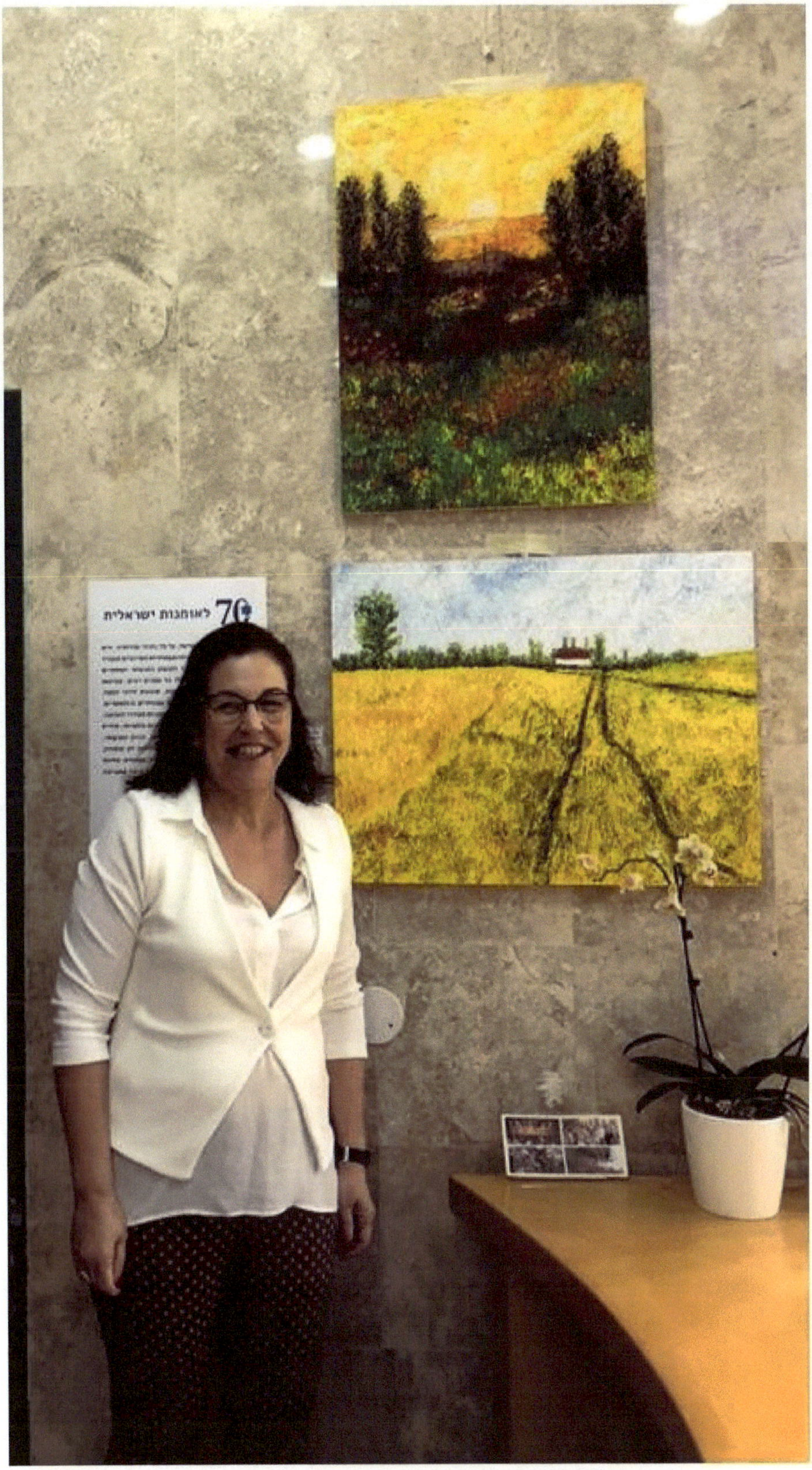

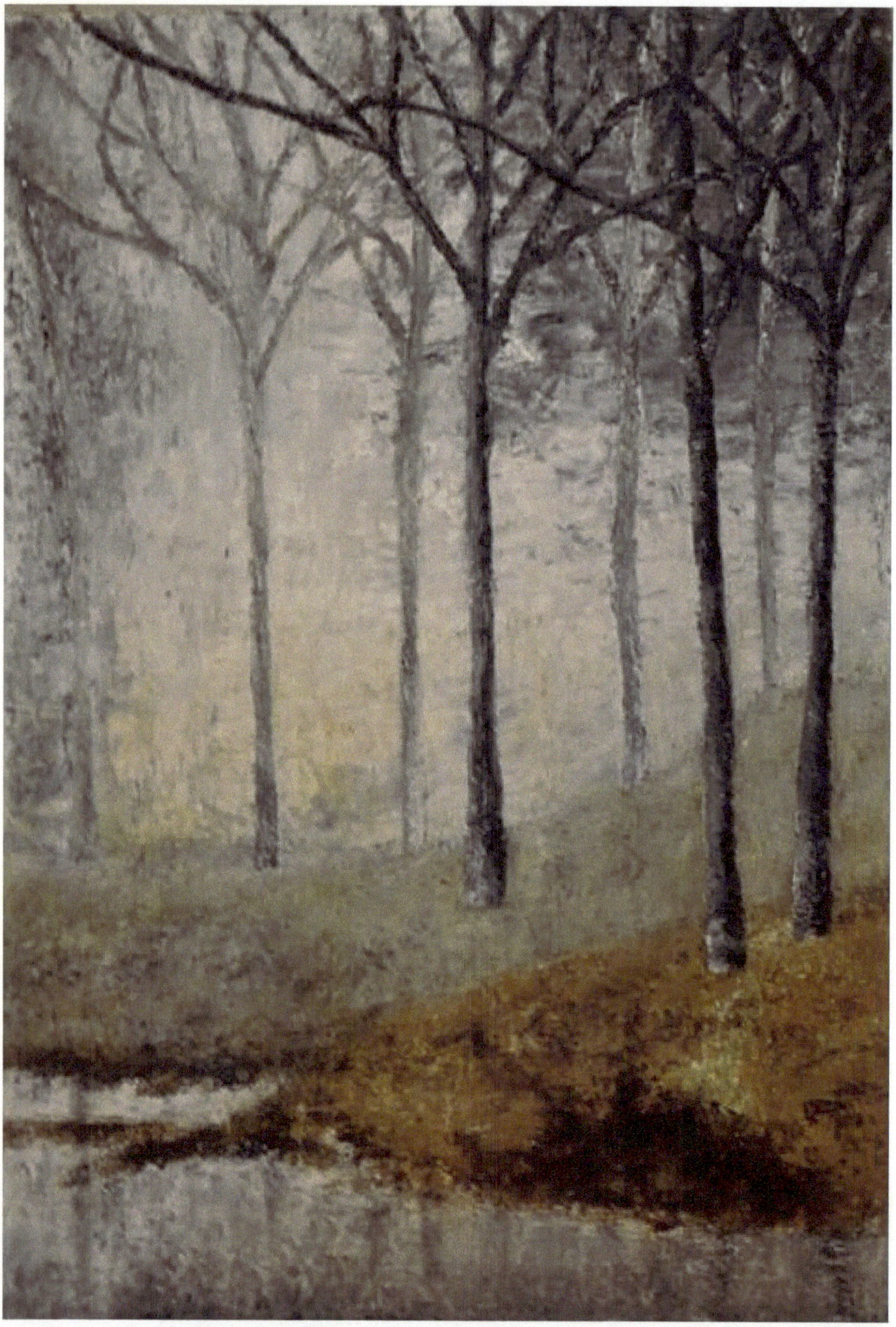

Oil on Special paper attached to a wood 70 by 50 cm

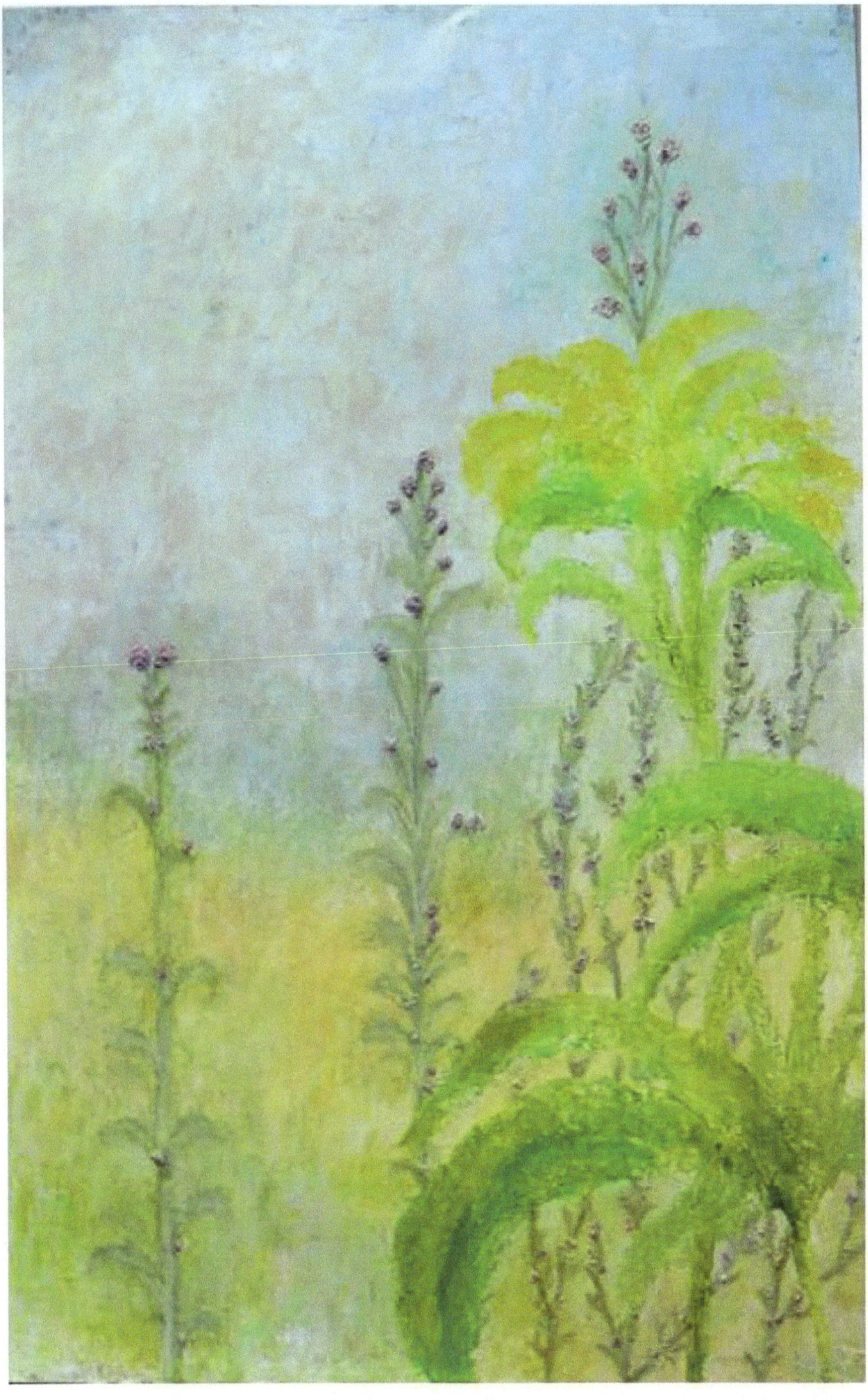

Oil on Special paper attached to a wood, 50 by 35 cm

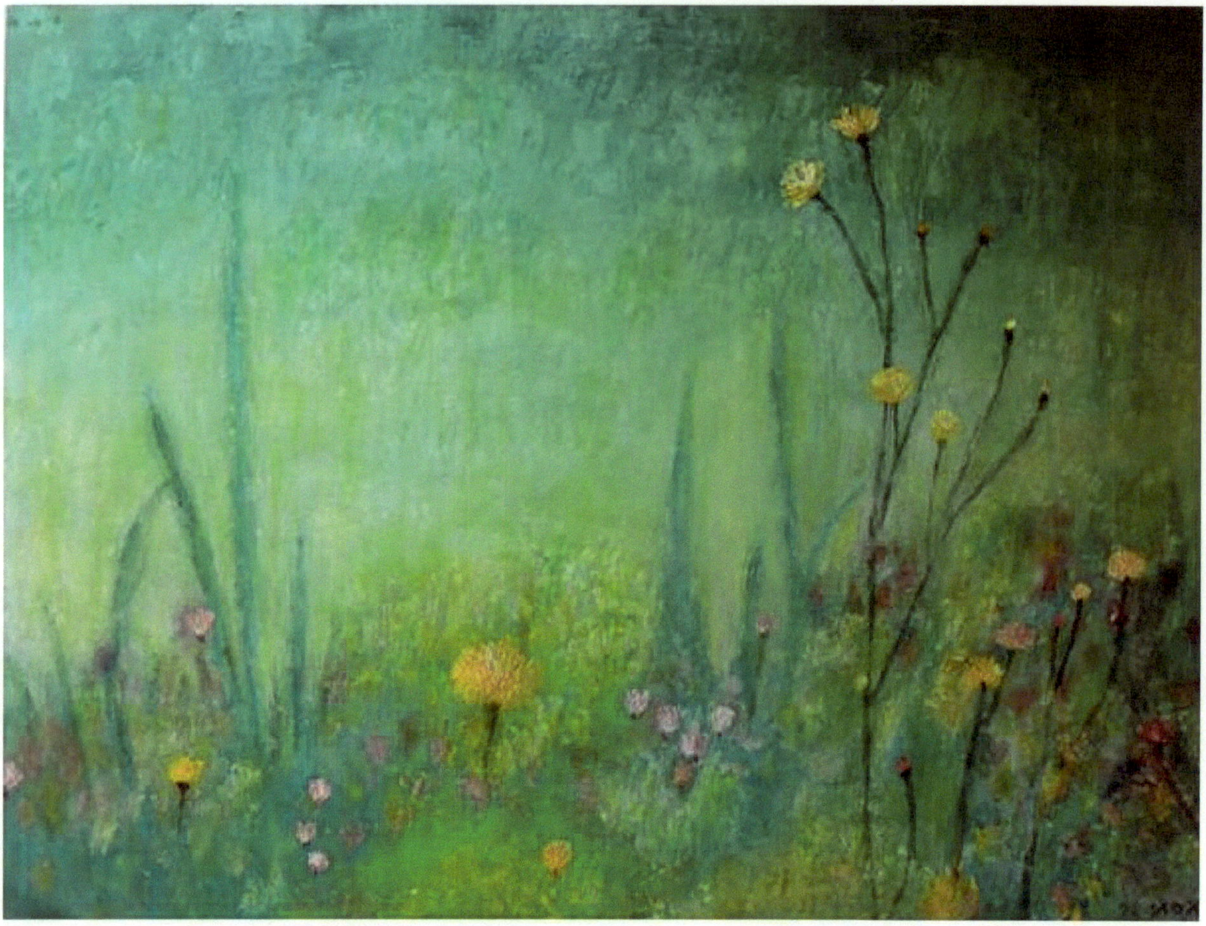

Oil on Special paper attached to a wood, 50 by 70 cm

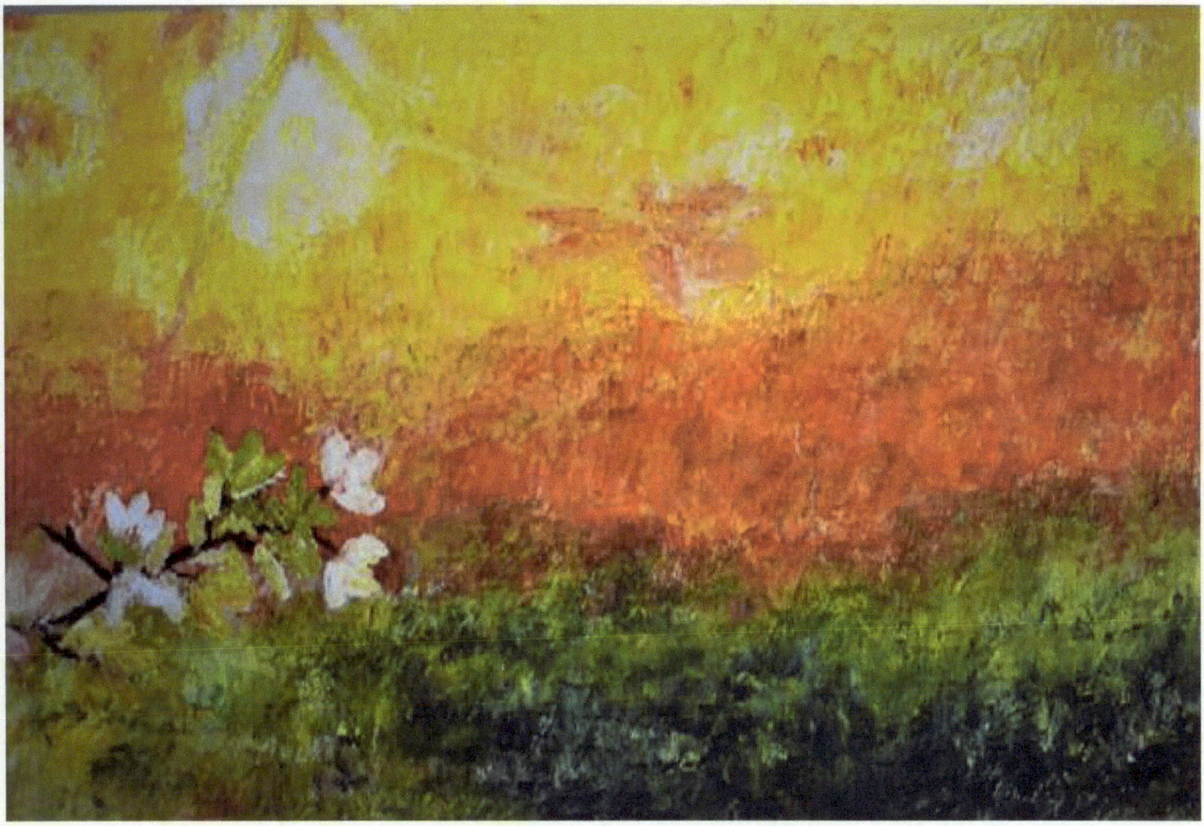

Oil on Special paper attached to a wood 35 by 50 cm

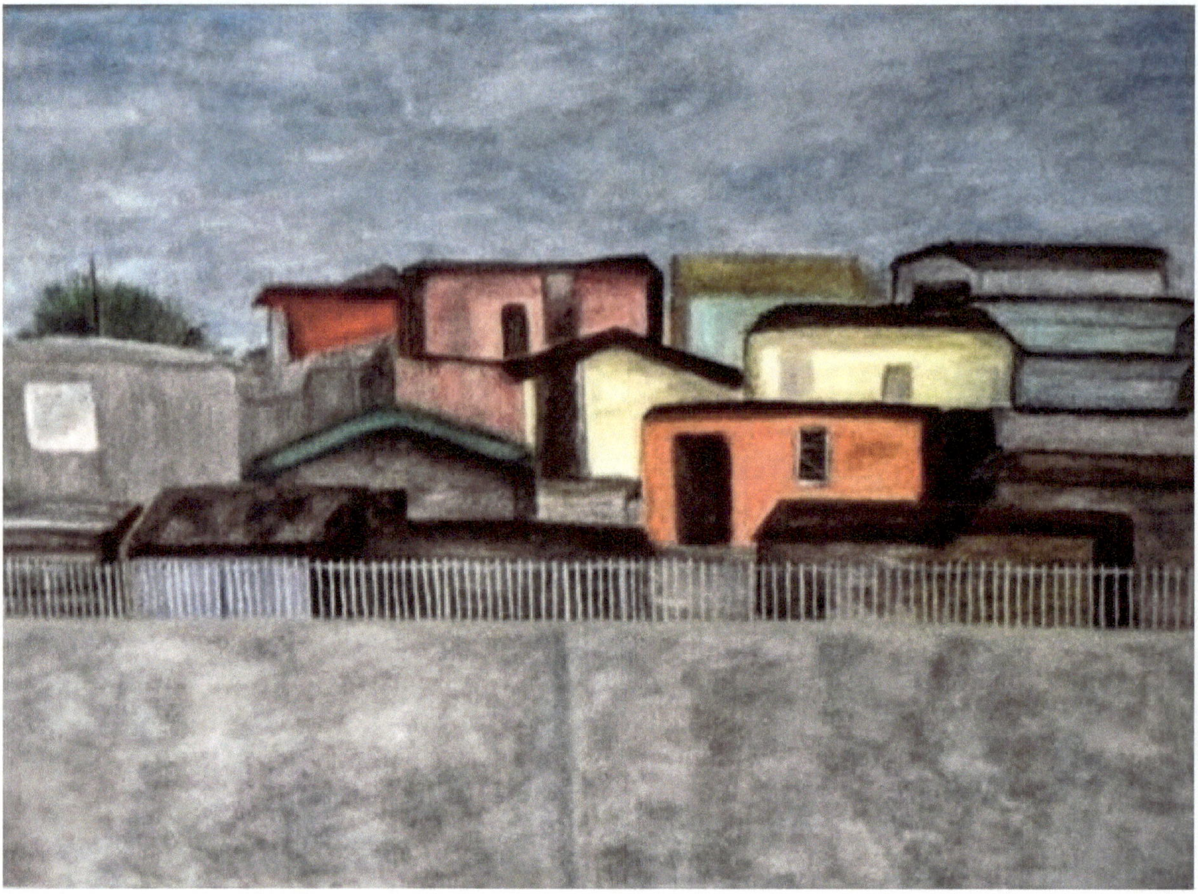

Oil on canvas 60 by 90 cm

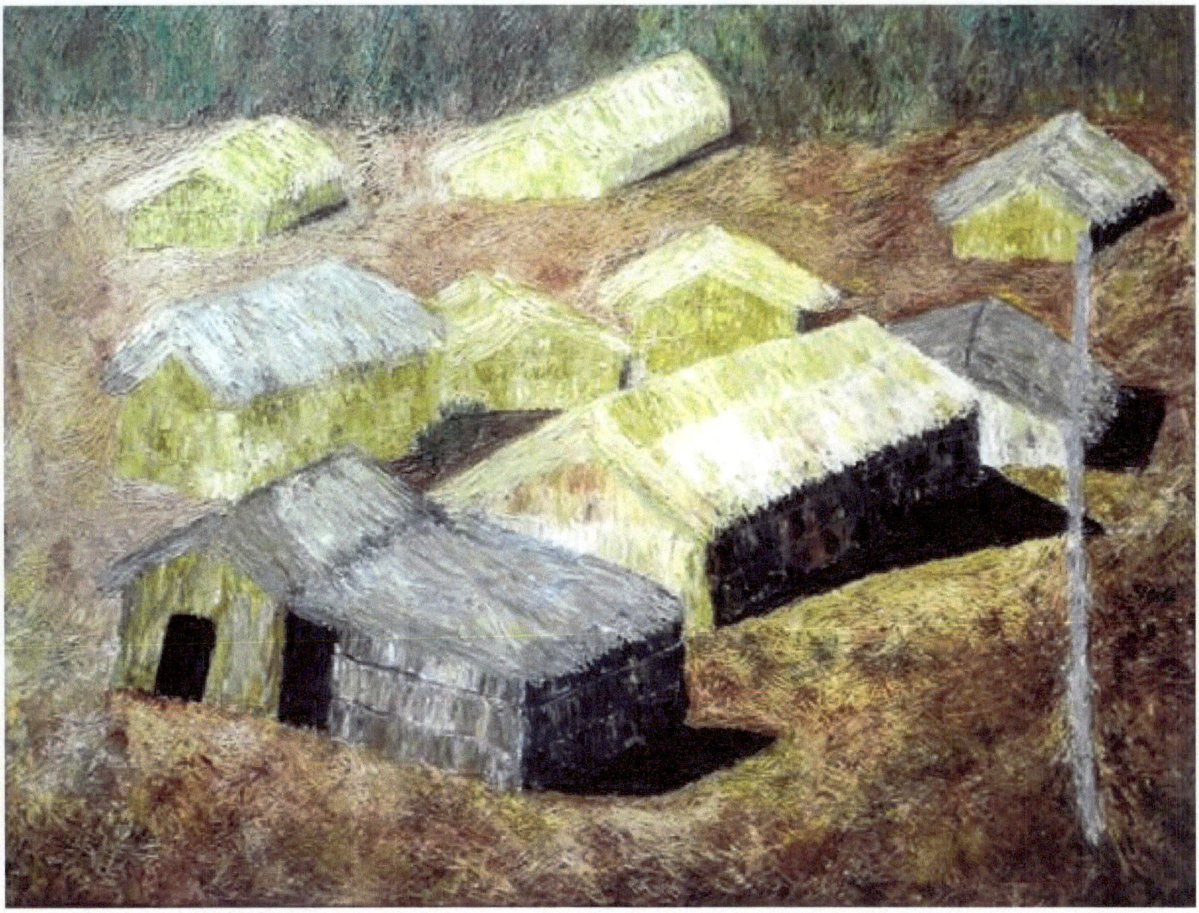

Oil on canvas 60 by 70 cm

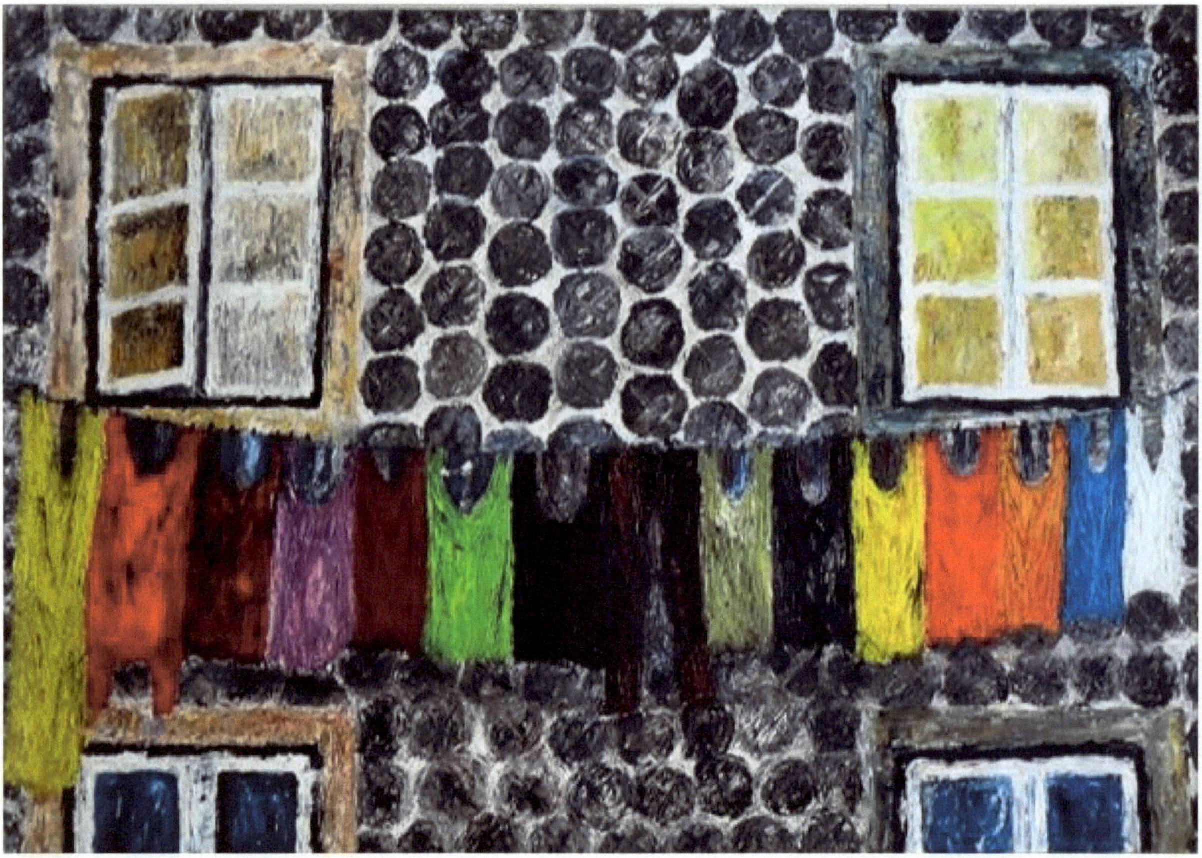

Oil on Lena paper attached to a wood 70 by 100 cm

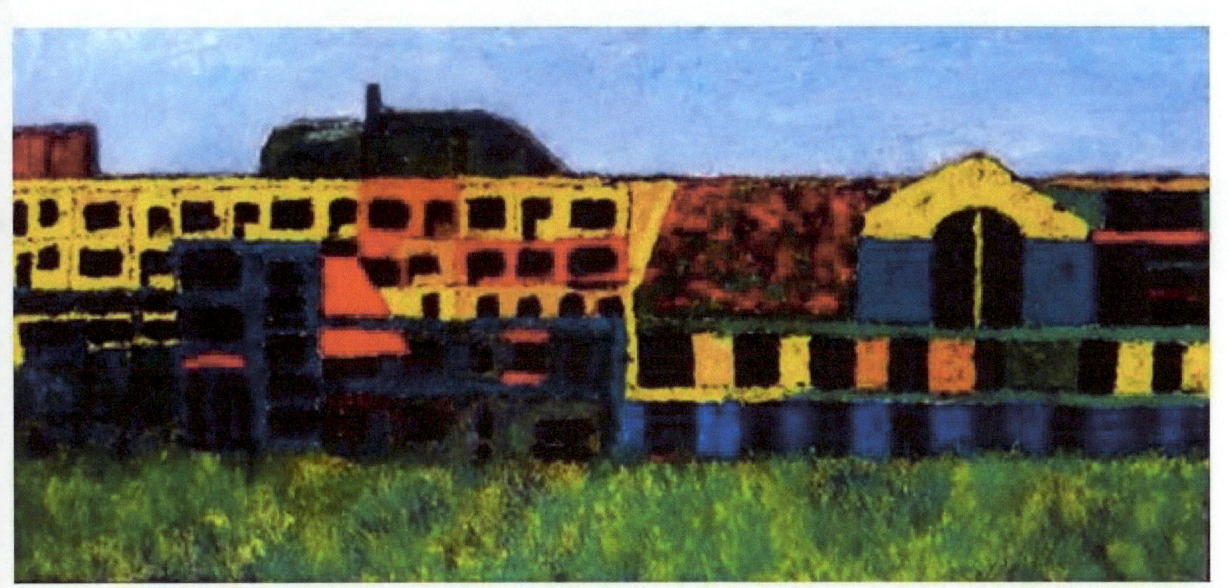

Oil on Special paper attached to a wood 40 by 100 cm

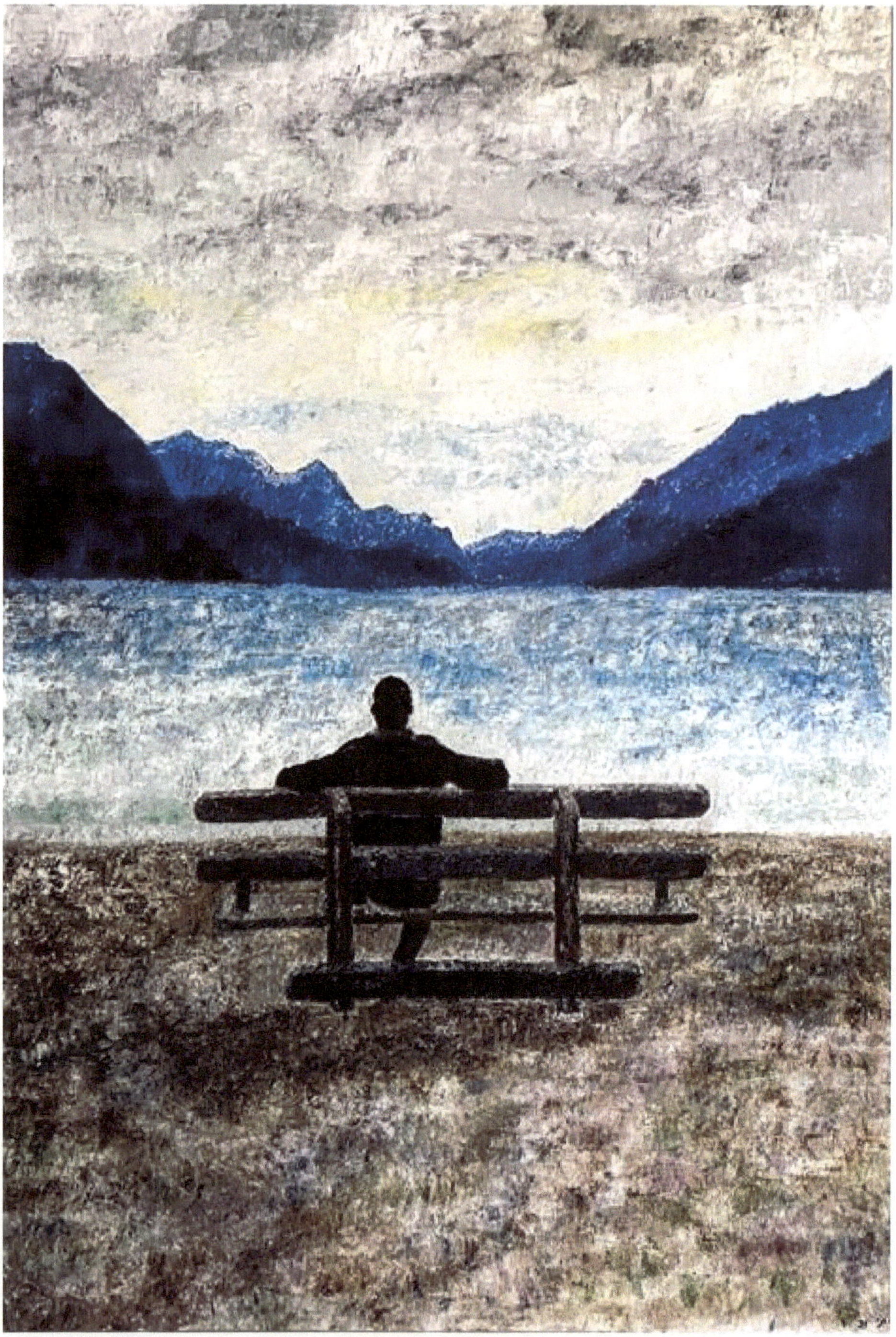

Oil on Special paper attached to a wood .100 by 70 cm

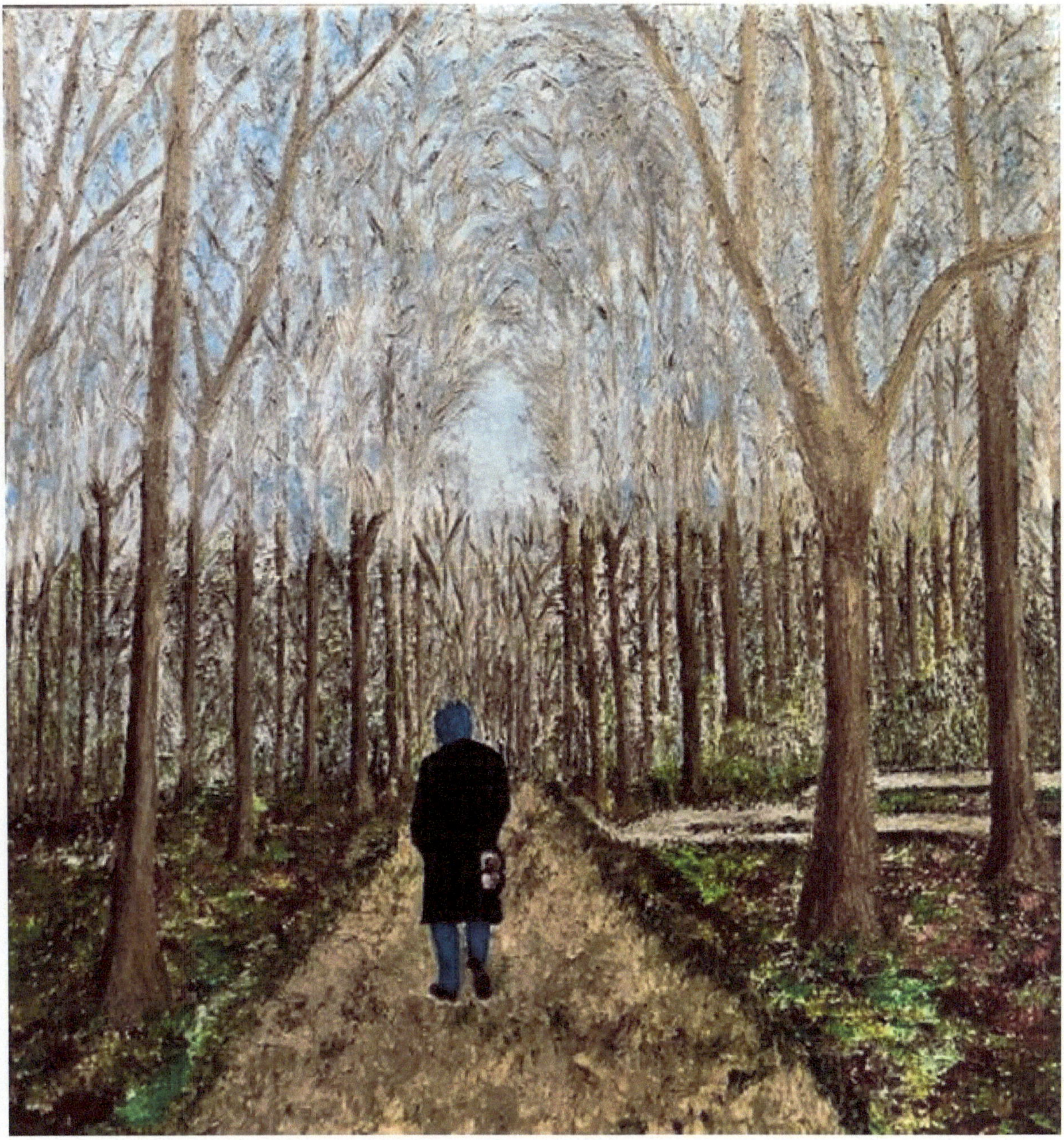

Oil on Special paper 90 by 90 cm

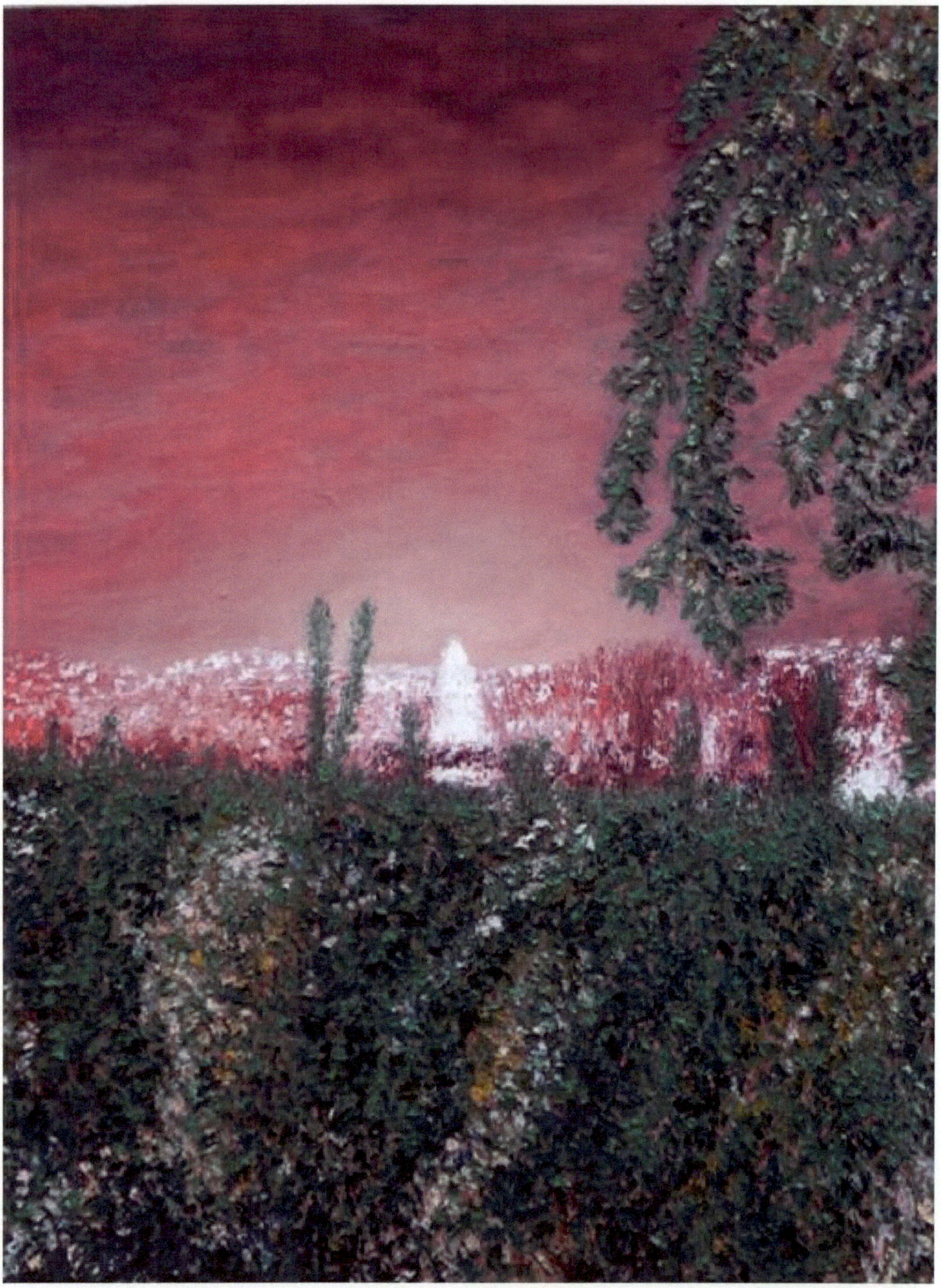

Oil on Special paper 70 by 50 cm

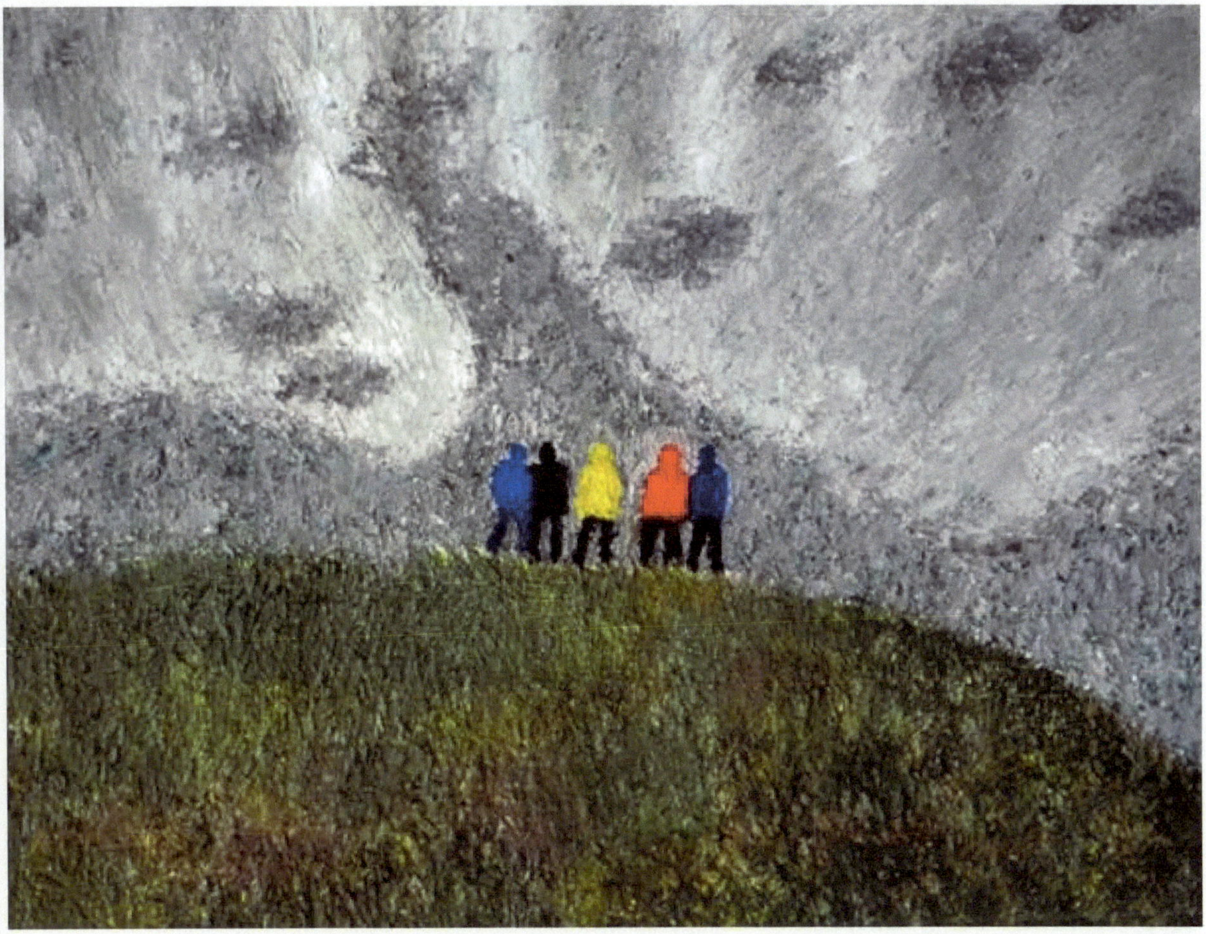

Oil on Special paper attached to a wood 50 by 70 cm

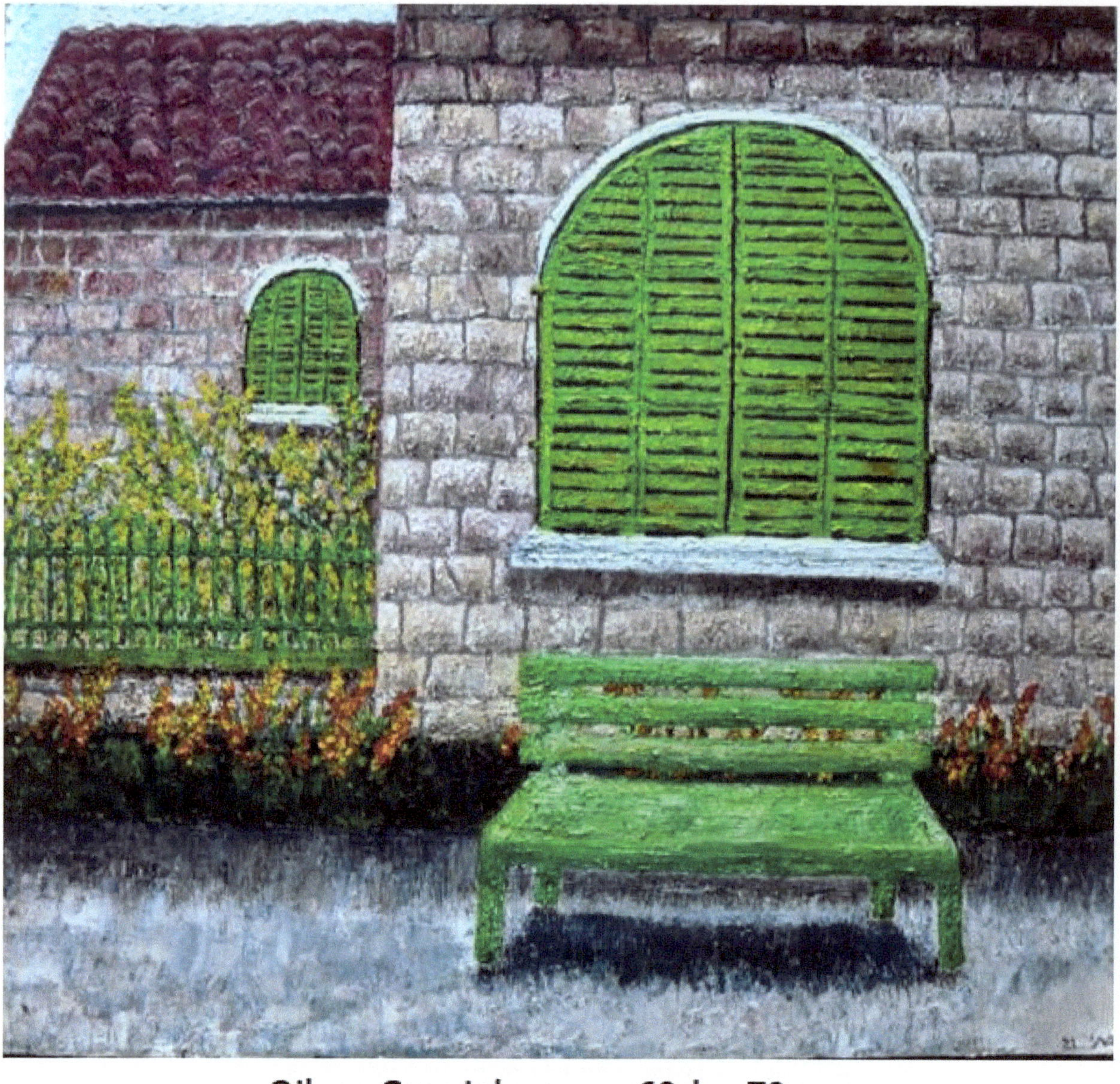

Oil on Special paper 60 by 70 cm

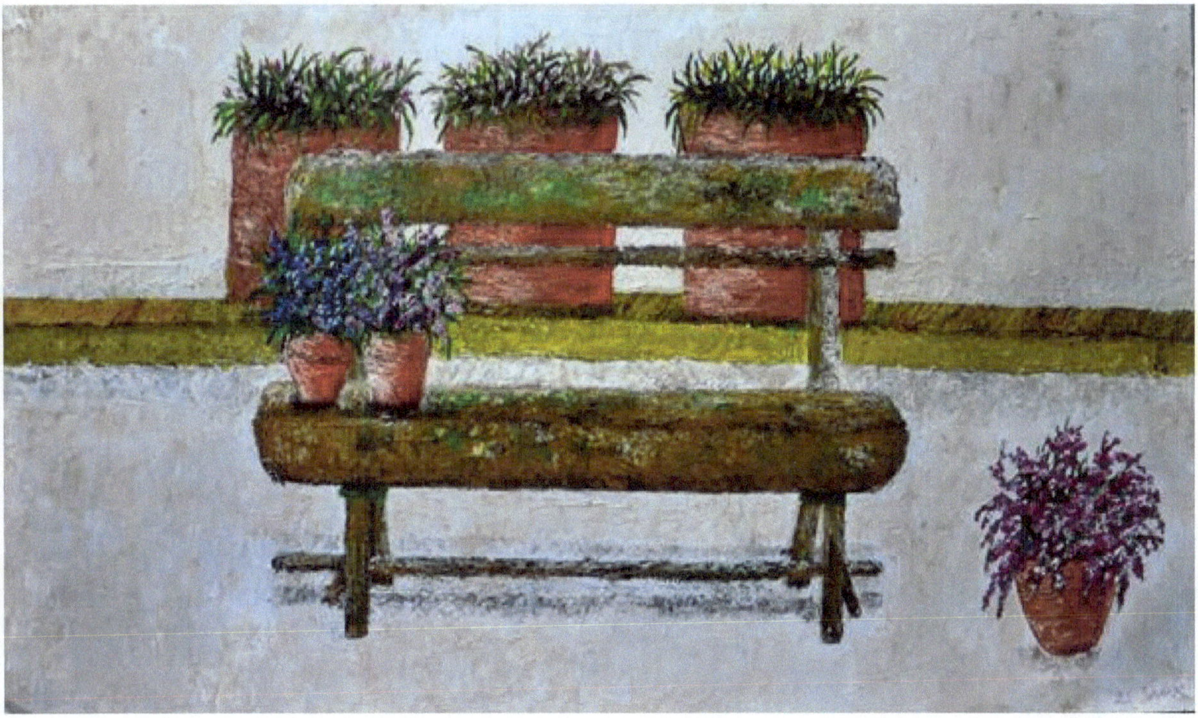

Oil on Special paper 40 by 70 cm

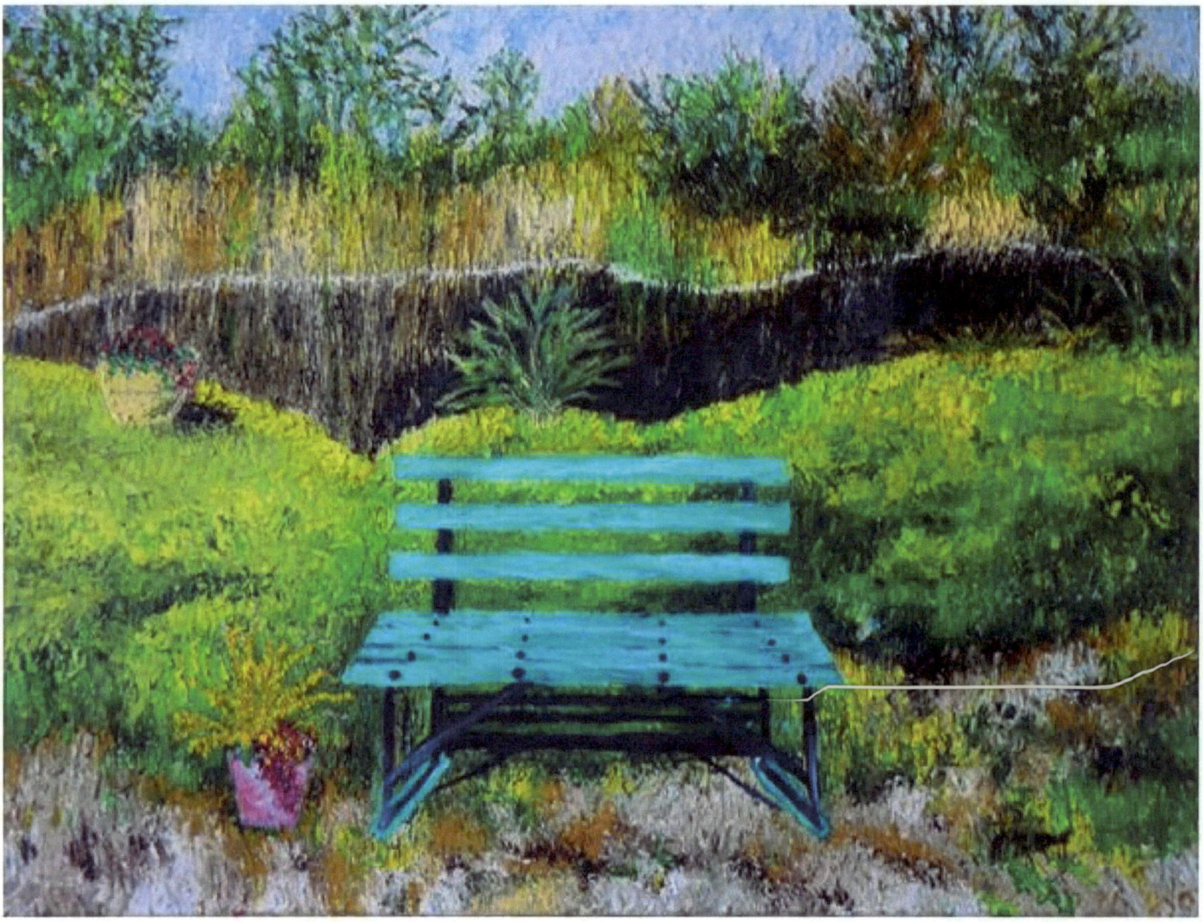

Oil on Special paper 50 by 70 cm

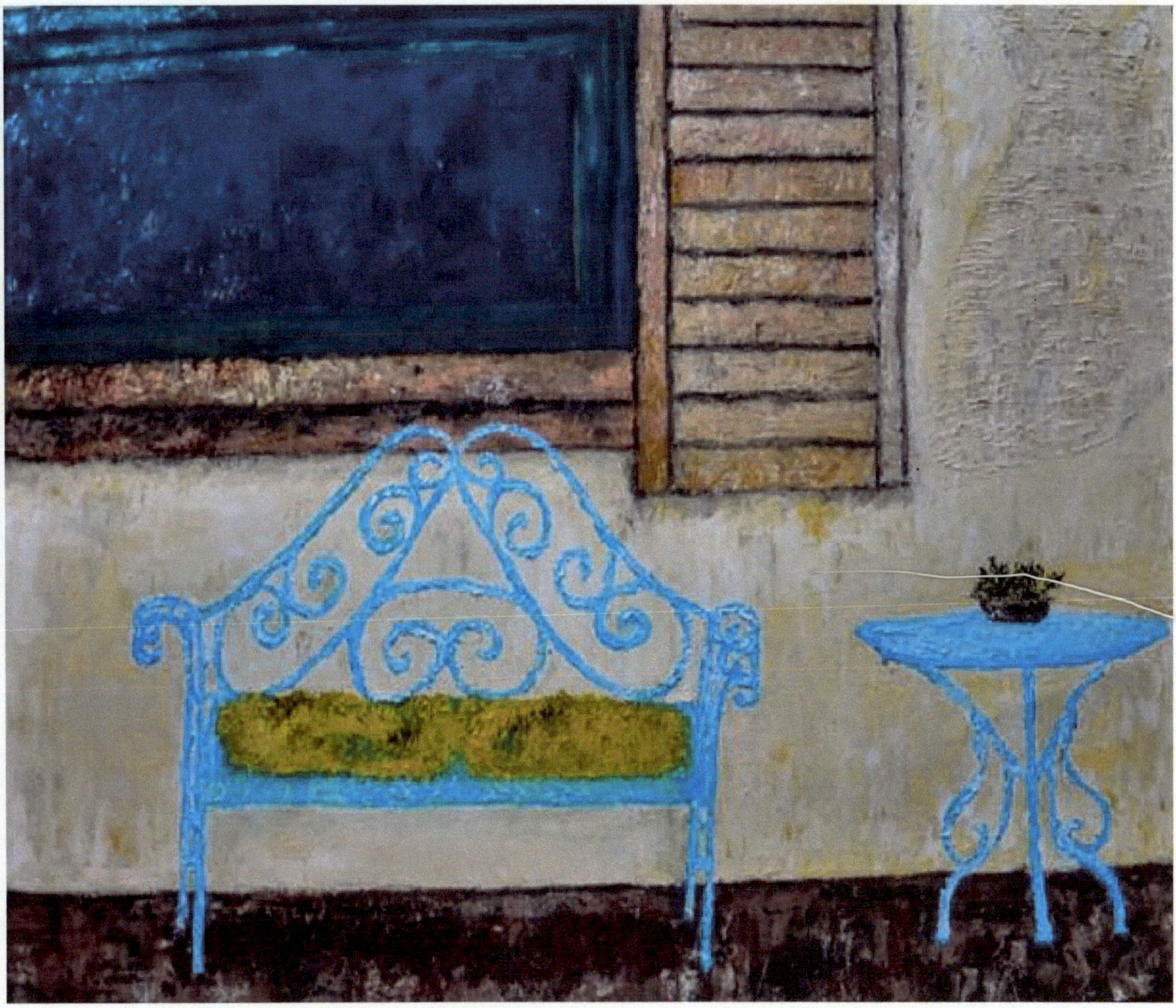

Oil on Special paper 60 by 70 cm

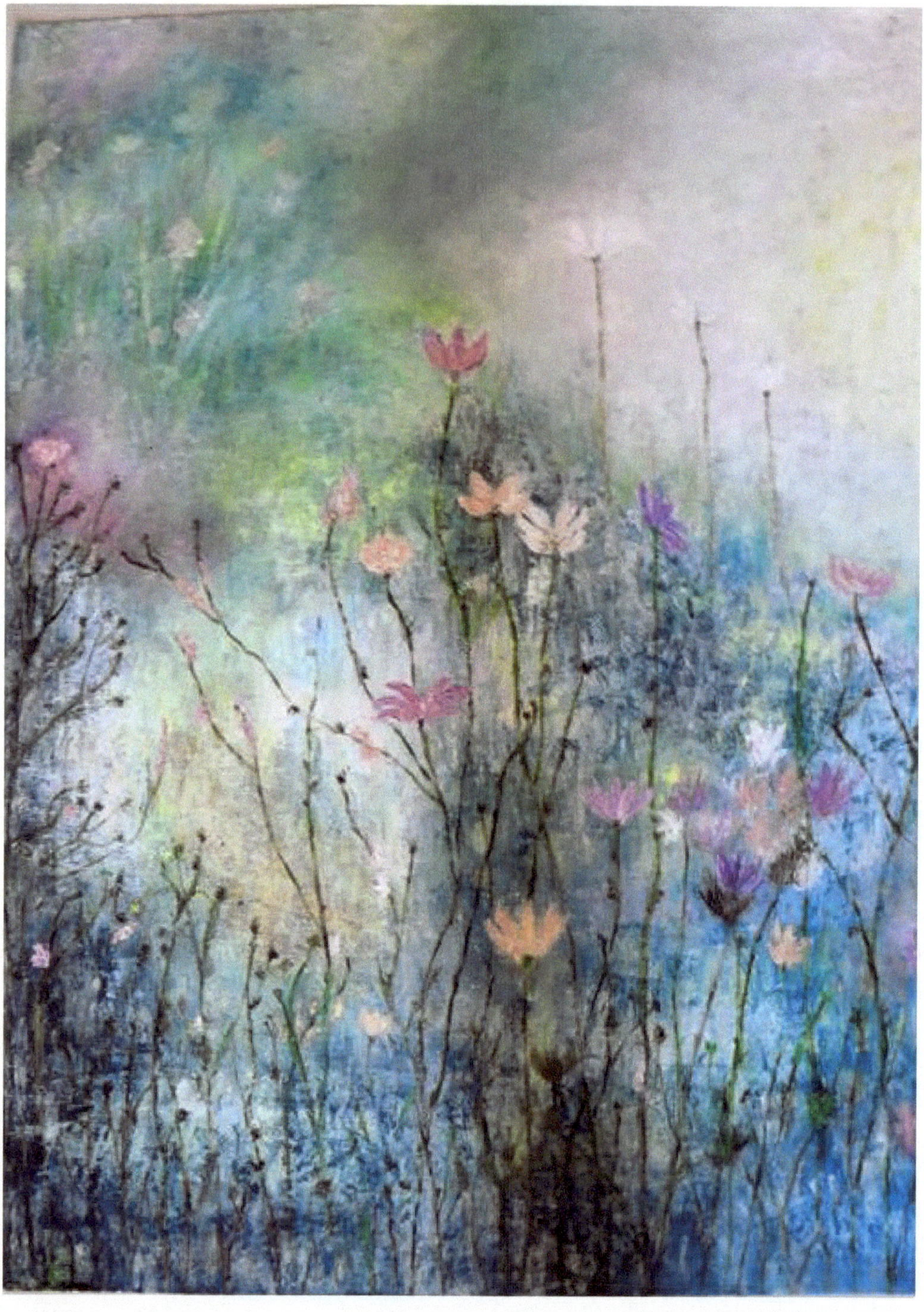

Oil on Special paper attached to a wood 70 by 50 cm

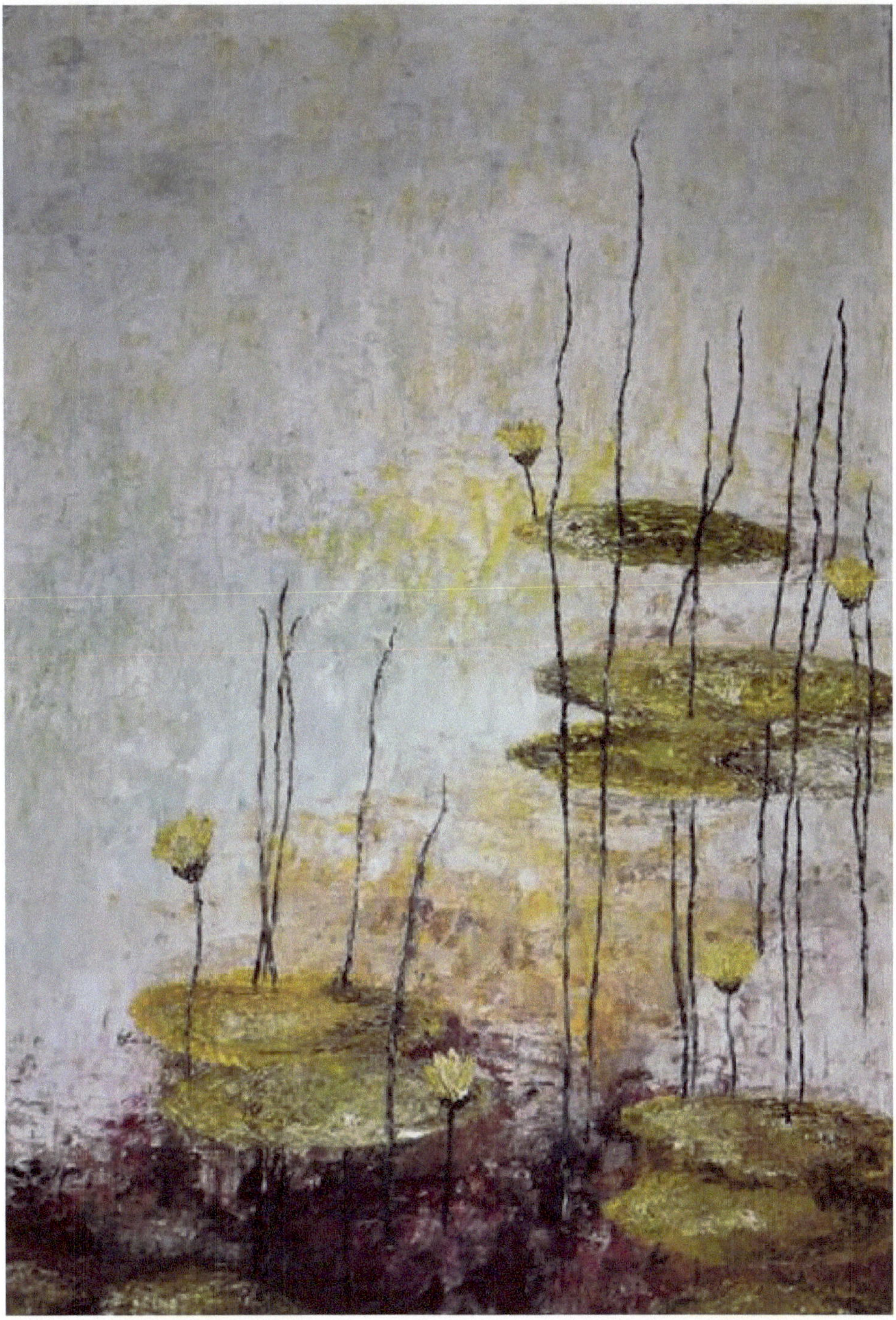

Oil on Special paper attached to a wood 70 by 50 cm

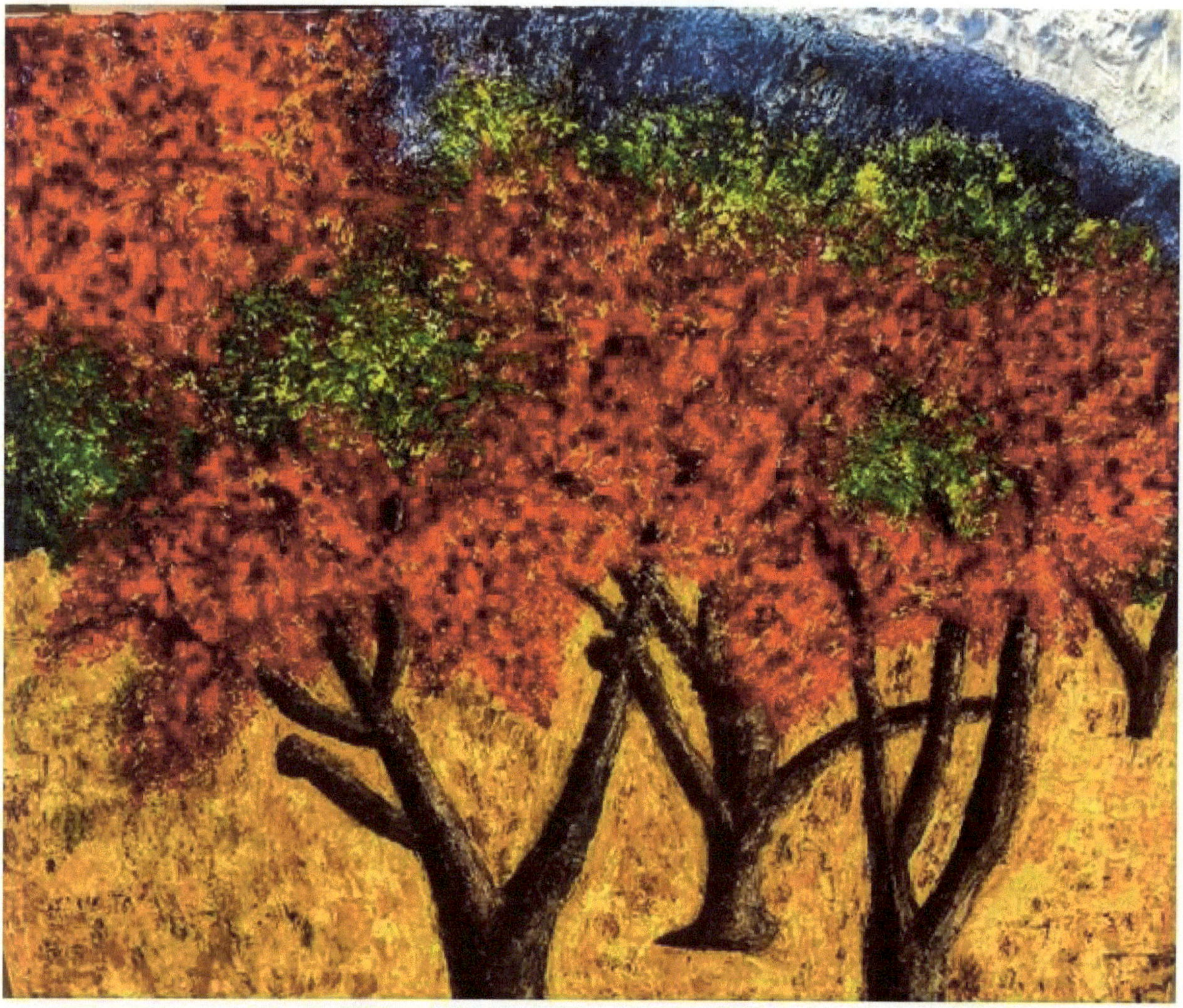

Oil on canvas 60 by 80 cm

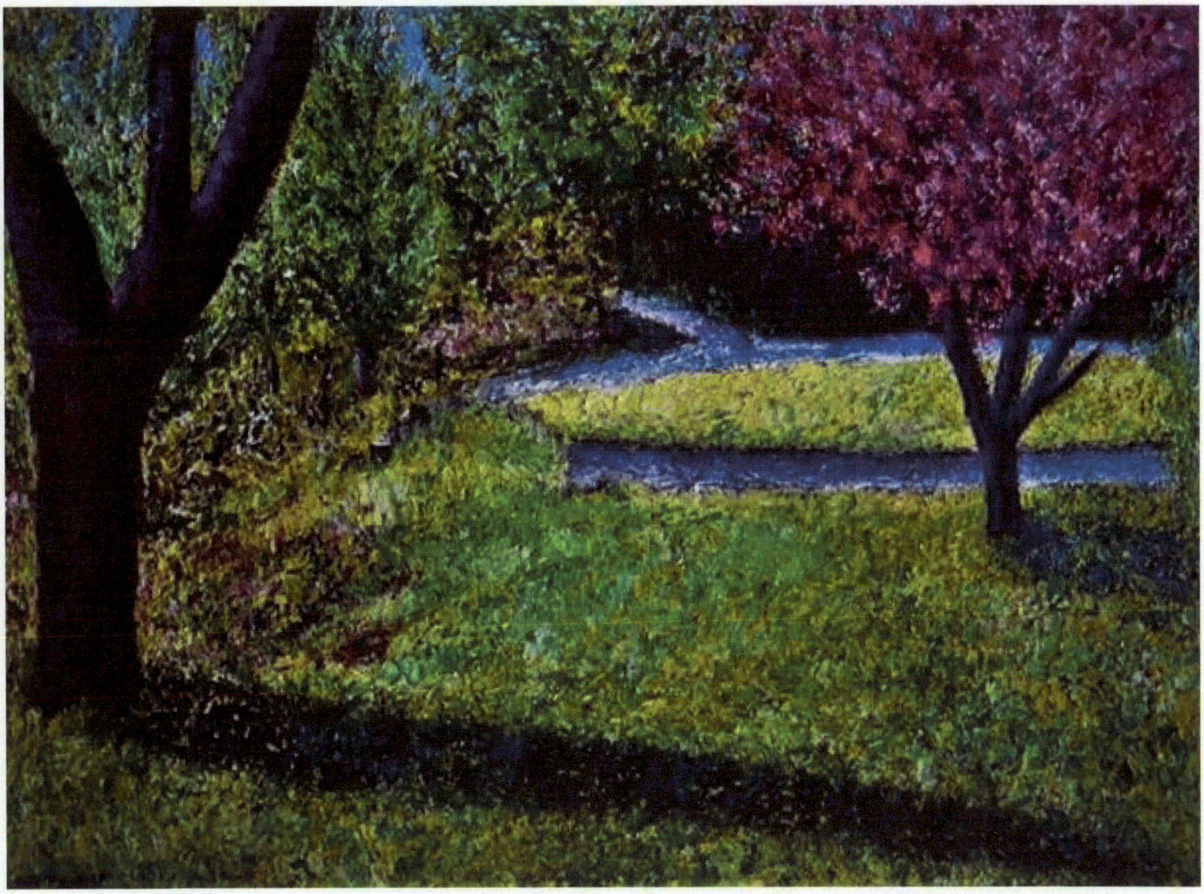

Oil on Special paper attached to a wood 50 by 70 cm

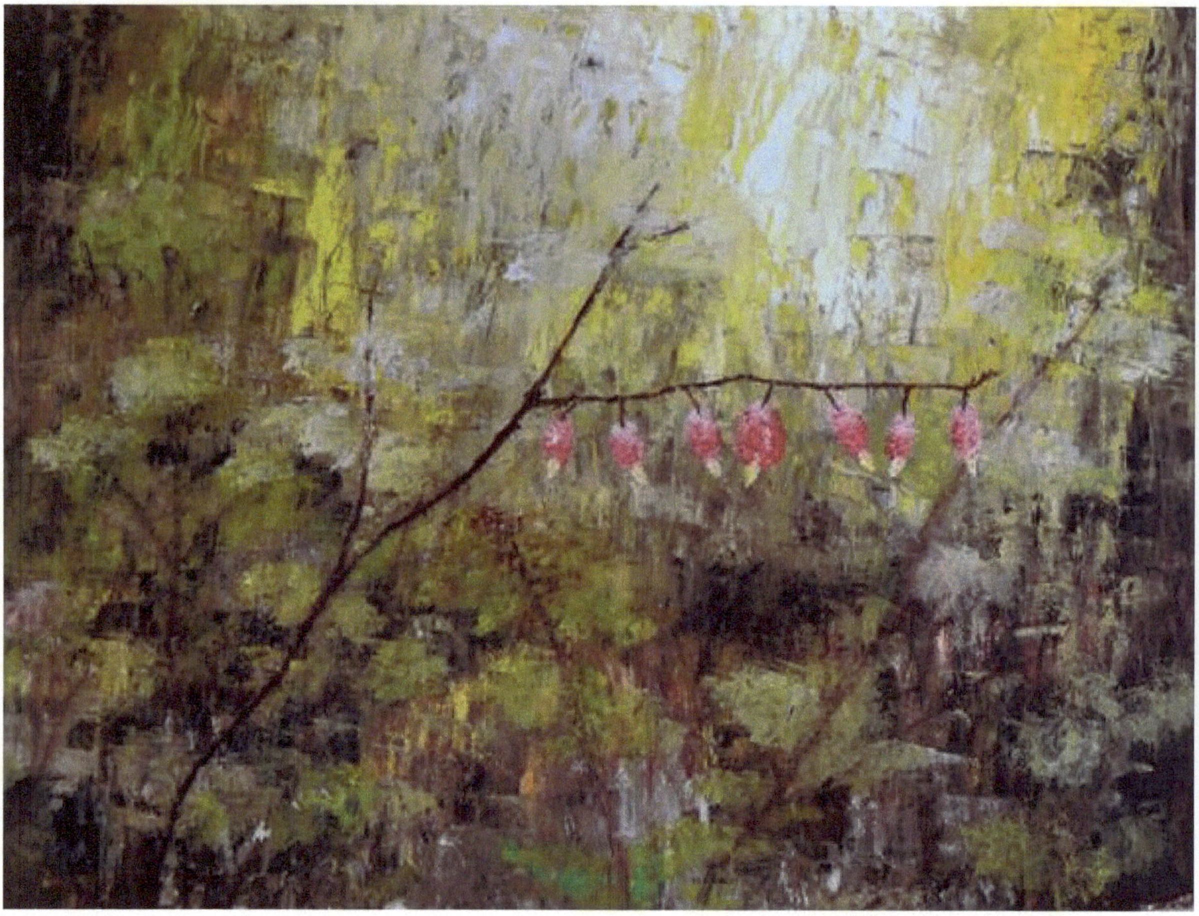

Oil on Special paper attached to a wood 50 by 70 cm

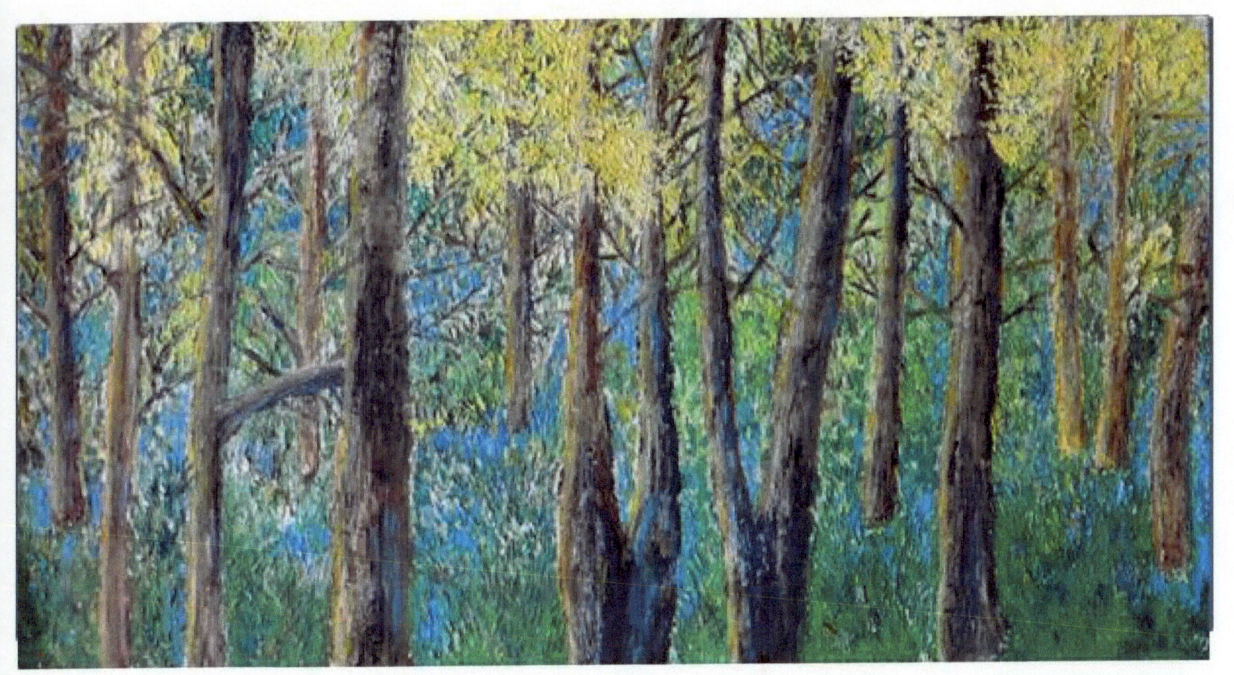

Oil on Special paper attached to a wood 55 by 100 cm

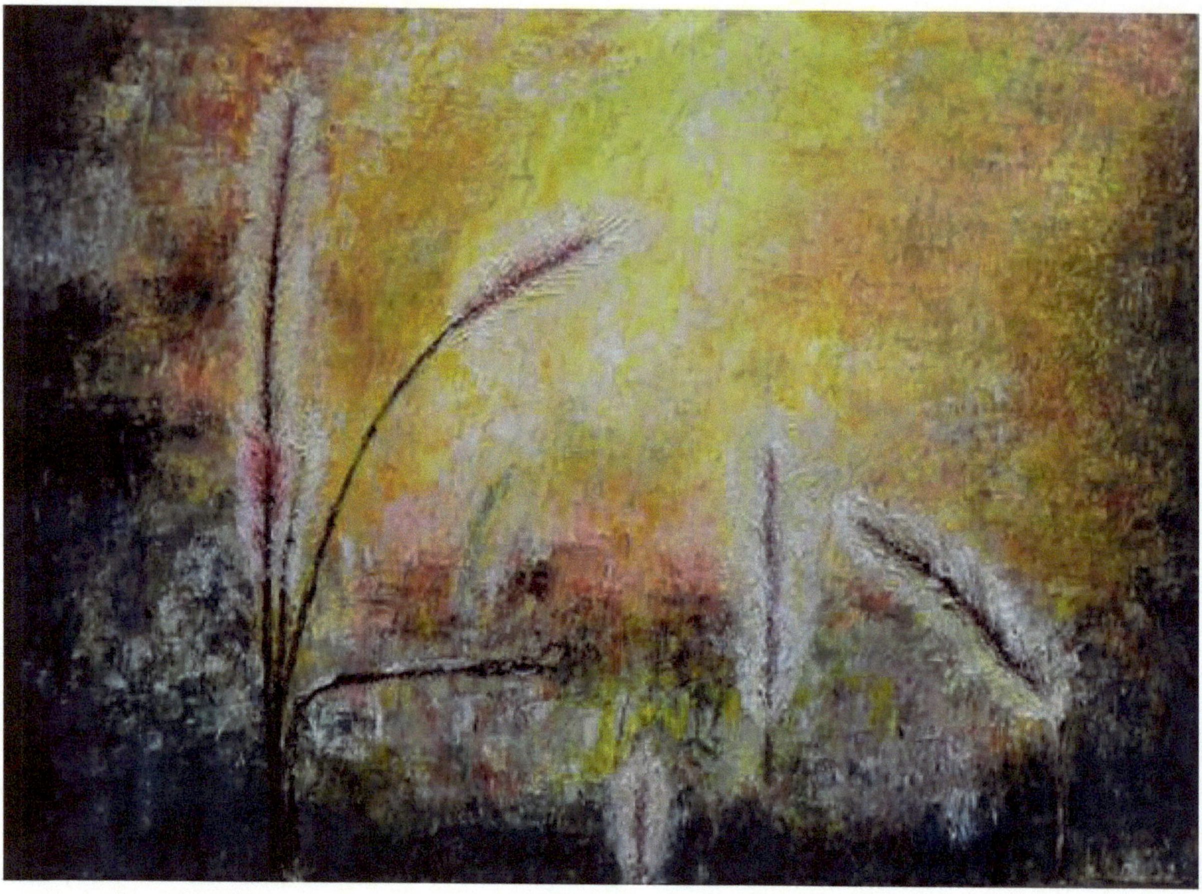

Oil on Special paper attached to a wood 50 by 70 cm

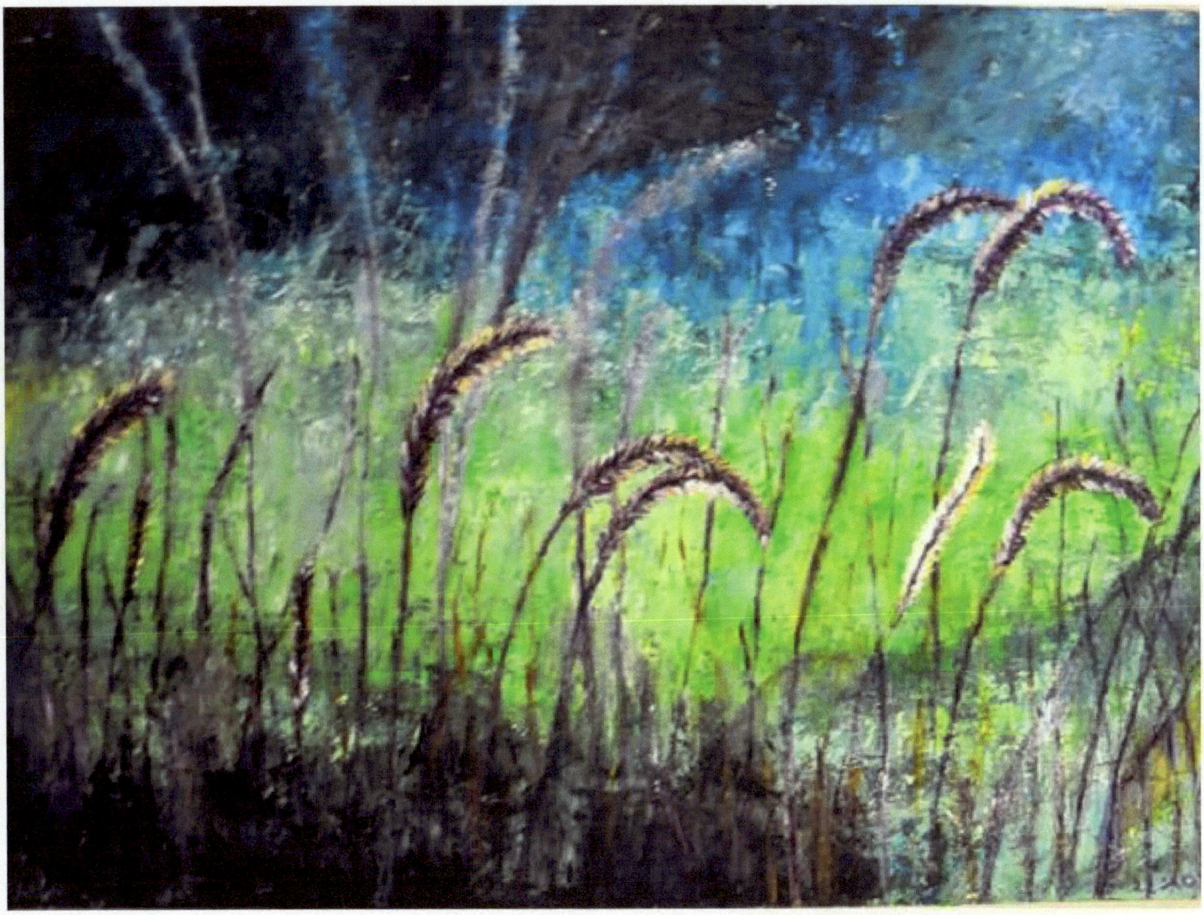

Oil on Special paper attached to a wood 35 by 50 cm

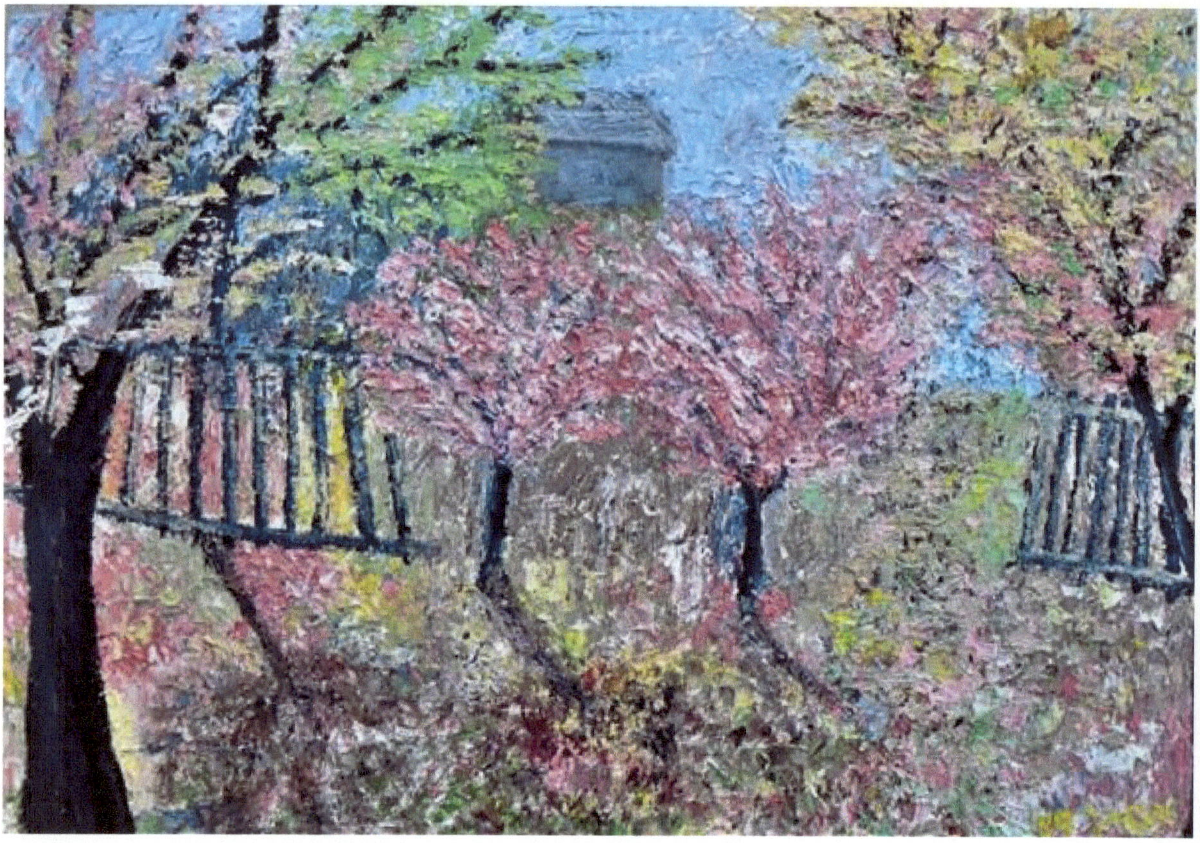

Oil on Special paper attached to a wood 30 by 45 cm

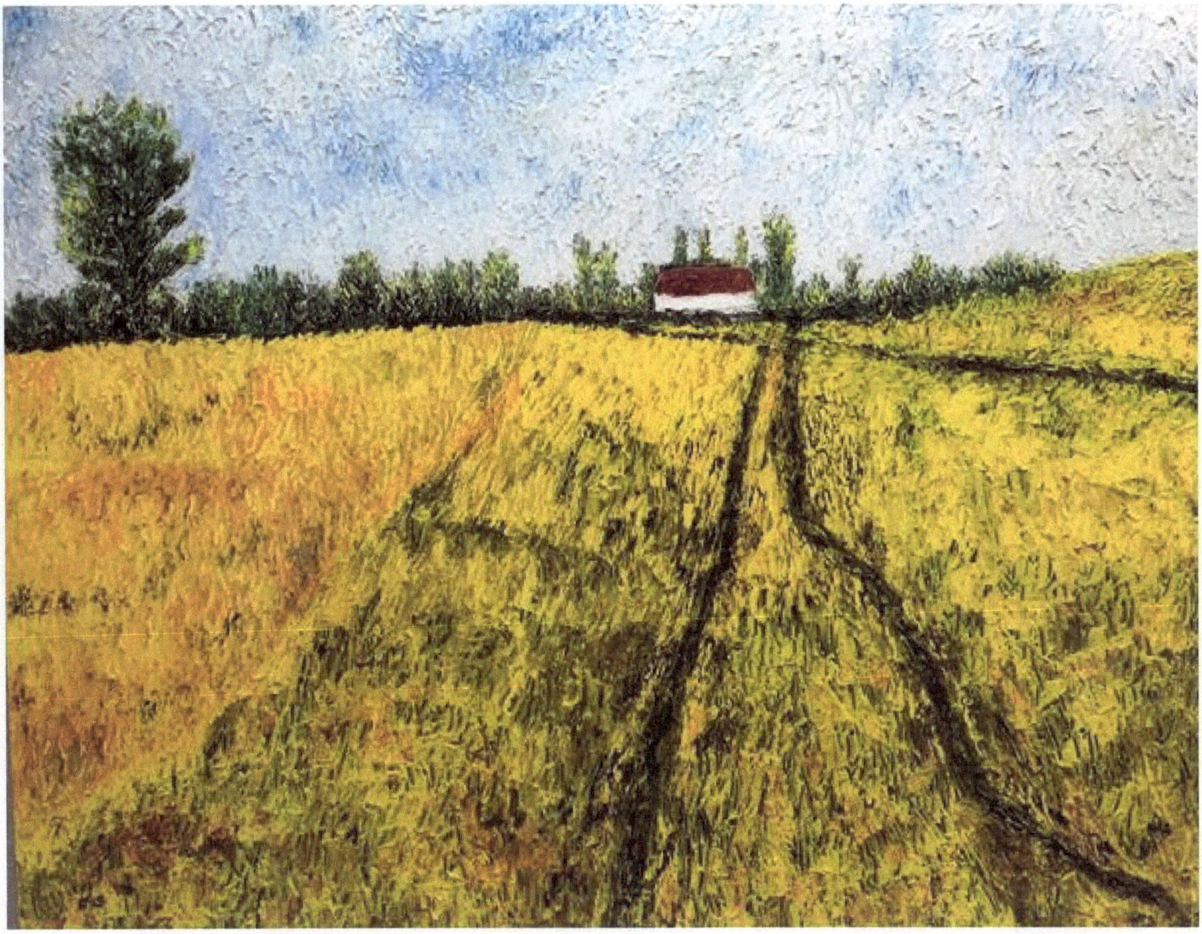

Oil on Special paper attached to a wood 50 by 70 cm

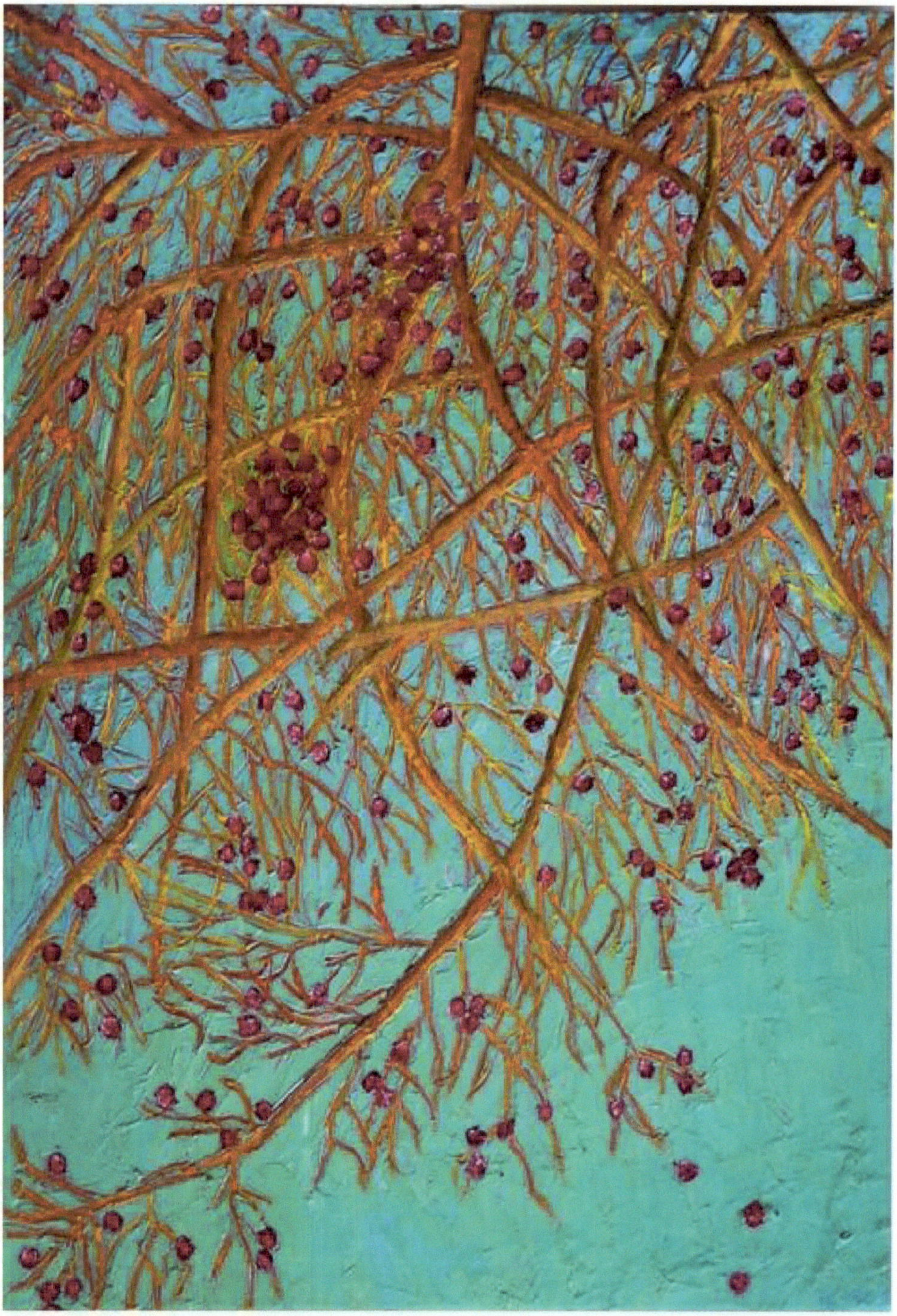

Oil on Special paper attached to a wood 70 by 50 cm

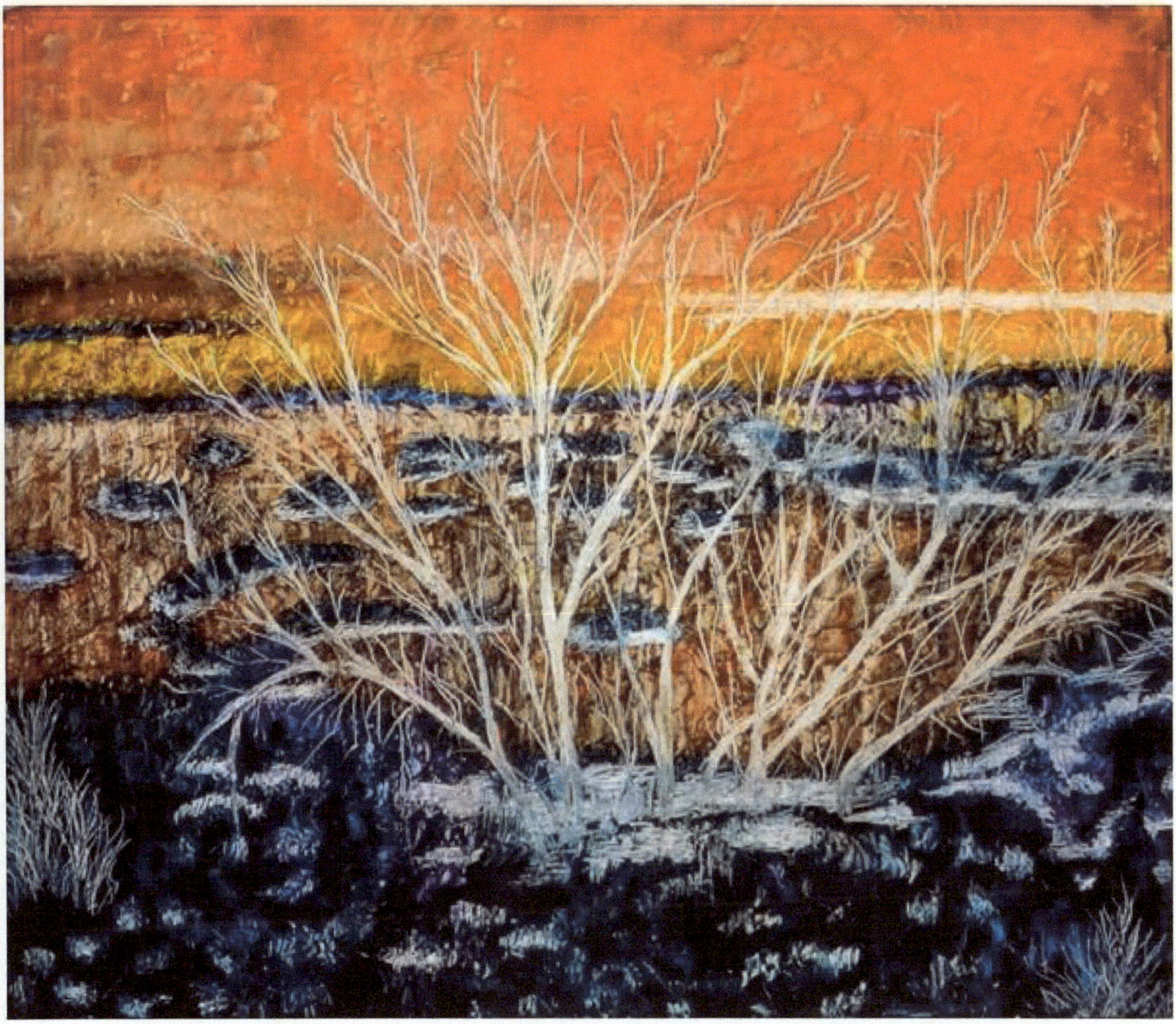

Oil on Special paper 60 by 70 cm

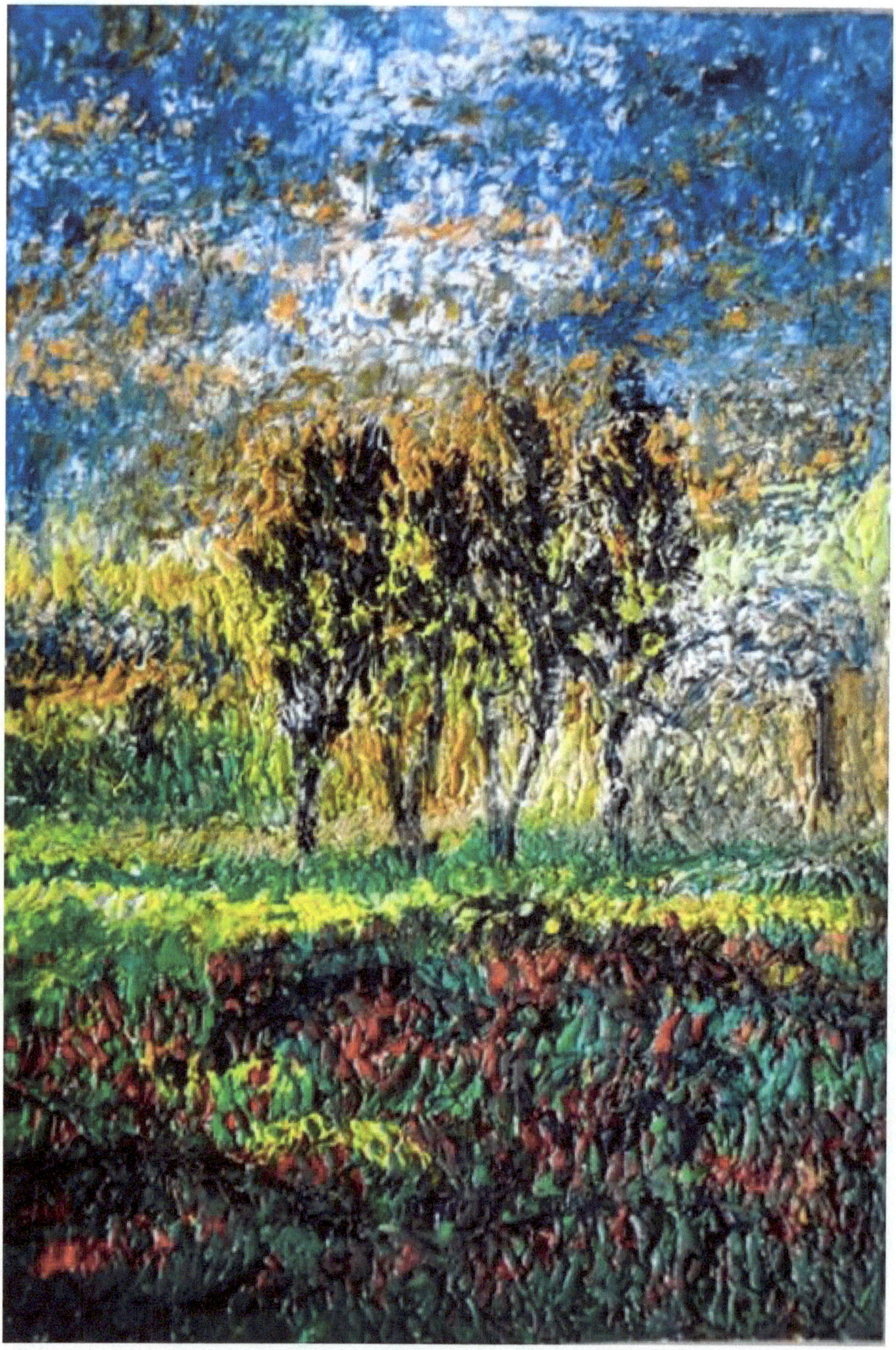

Oil on Special paper attached to a wood 34 by 23 cm

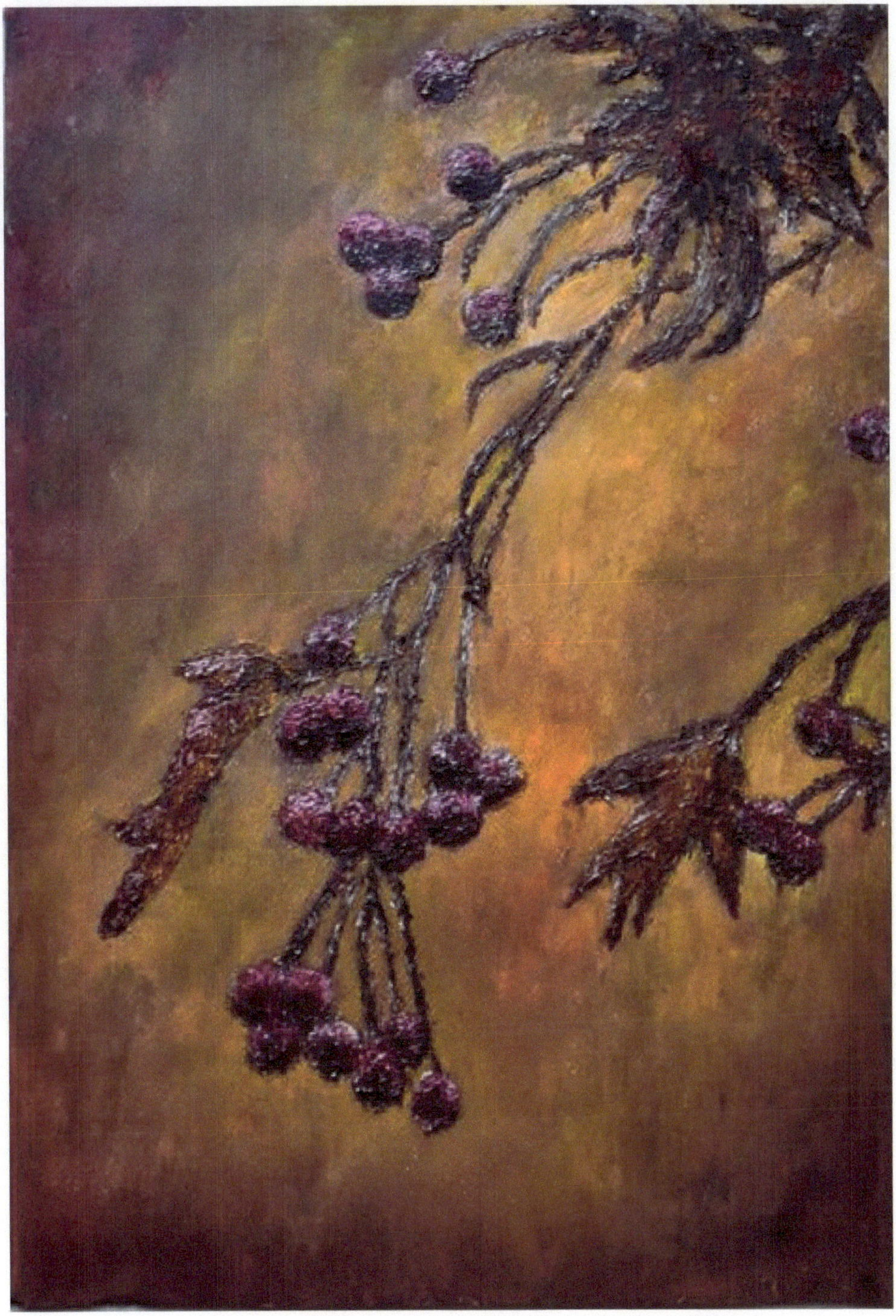

Oil on Special paper attached to a wood 50 by 35 cm

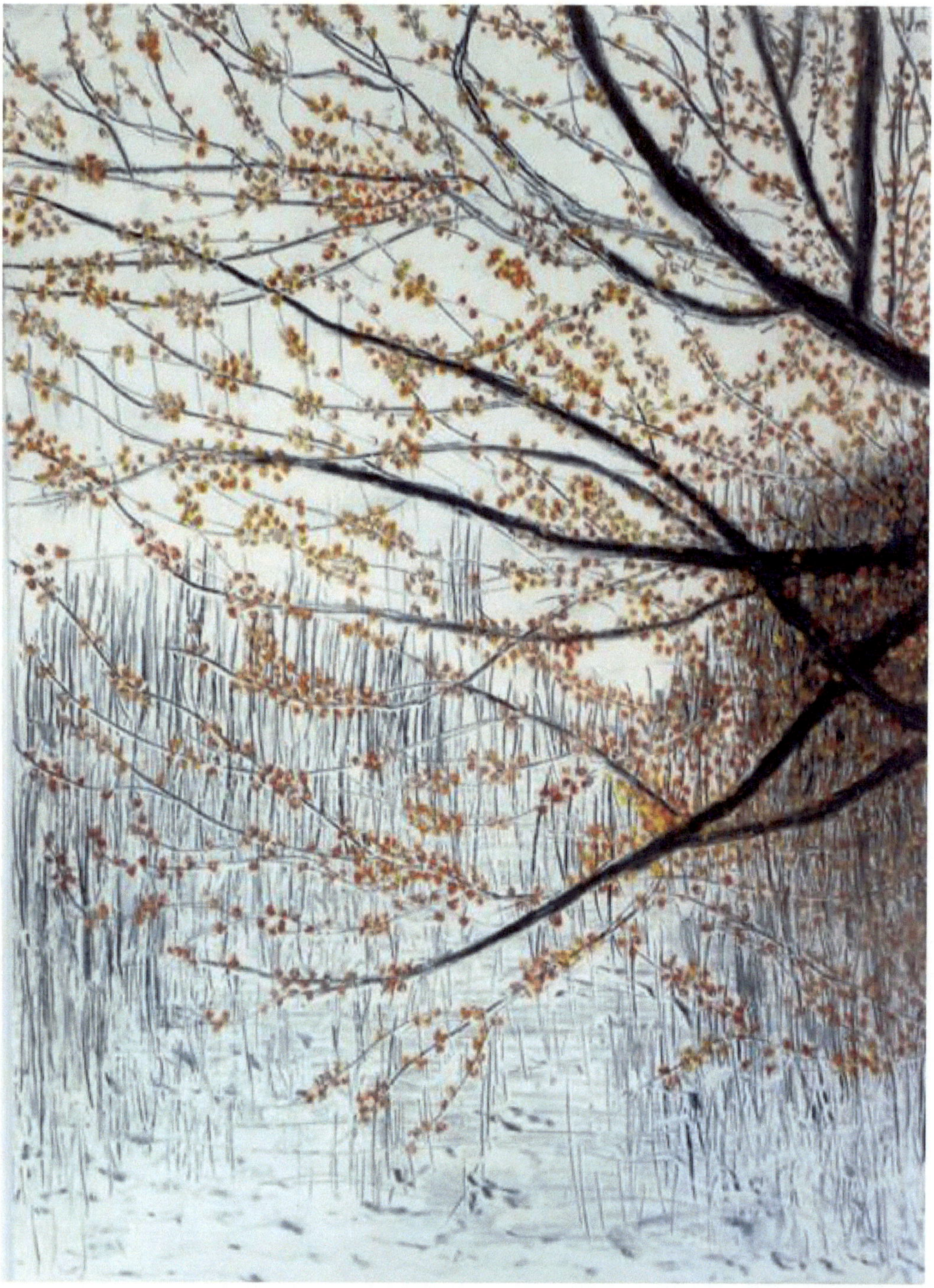

Oil on Special paper attached to a wood 60 by 40 cm

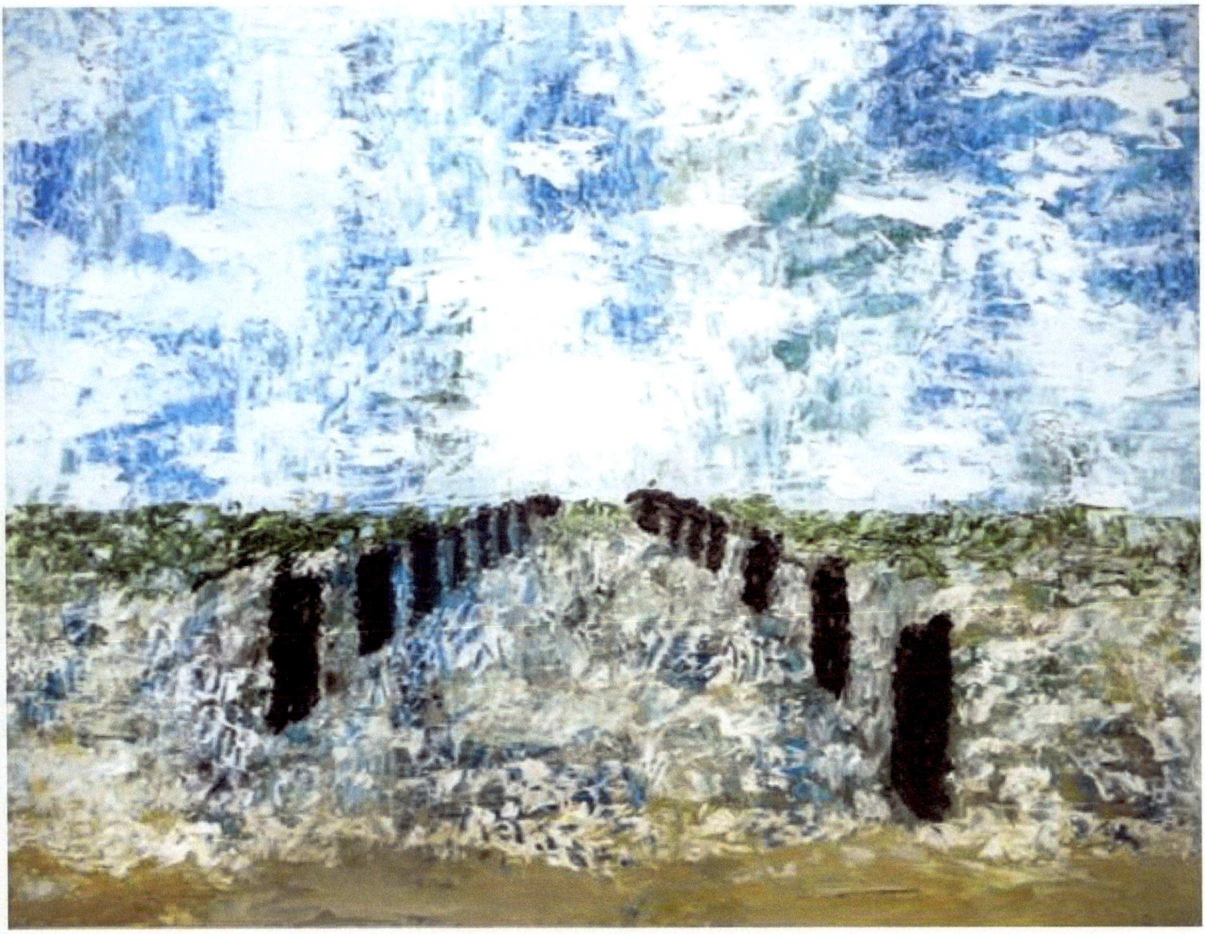

Oil on Special paper attached to a wood 40 by 60 cm

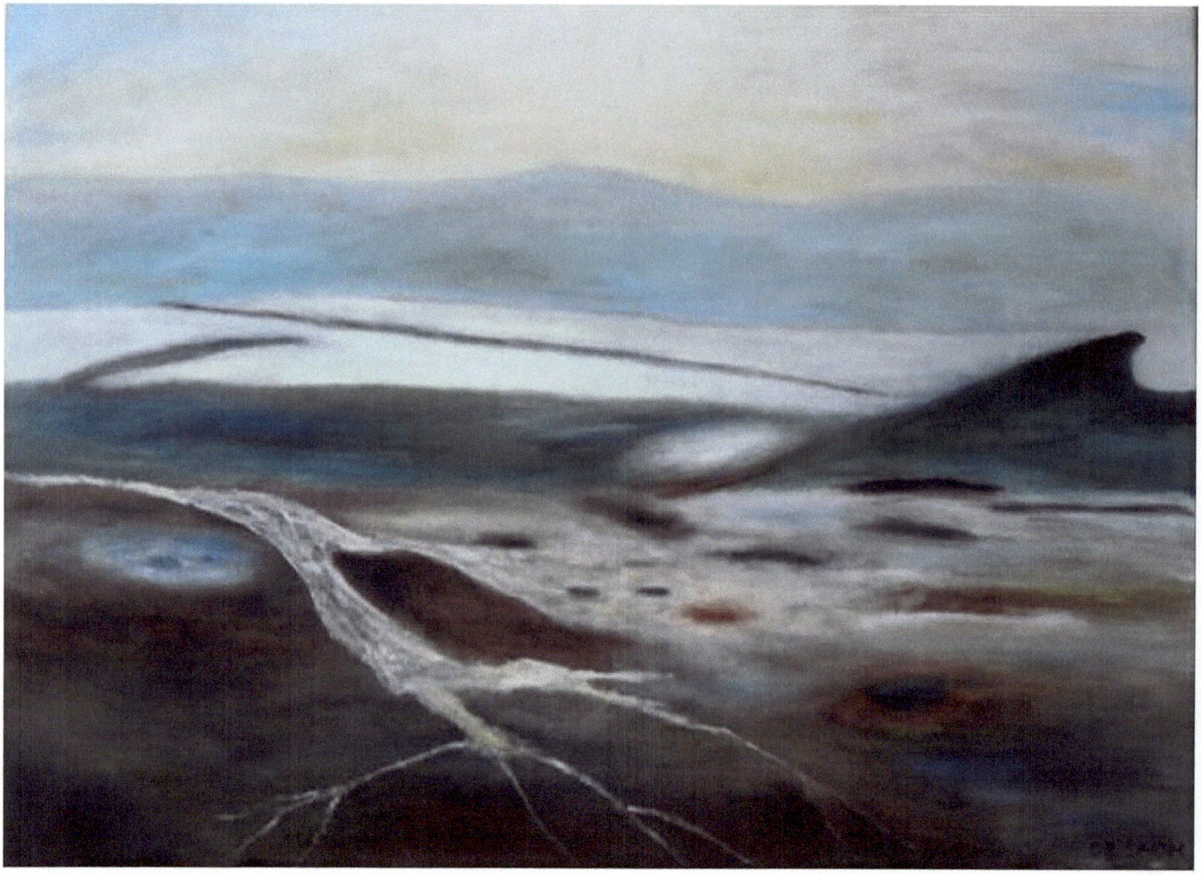

Oil on canvas 50 by 70 cm

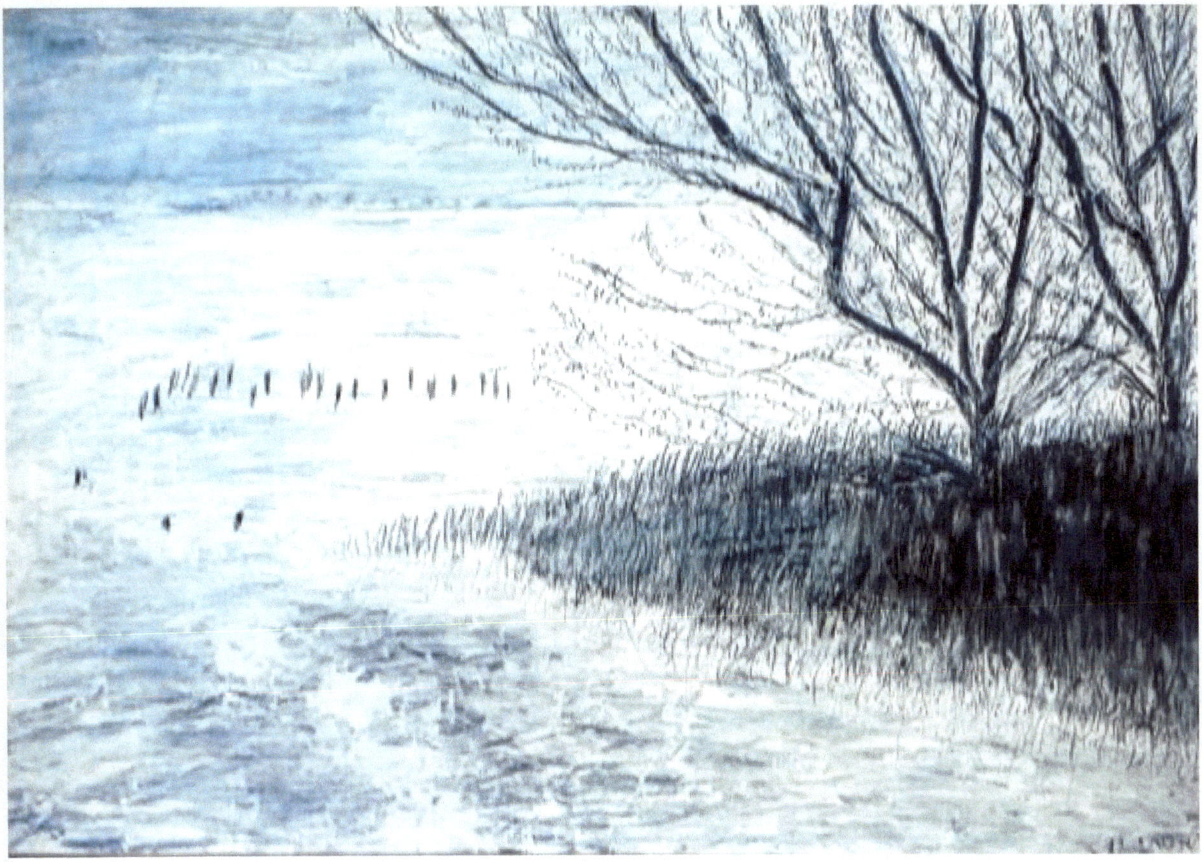

Oil on Special paper attached to a wood 40 by 60 cm

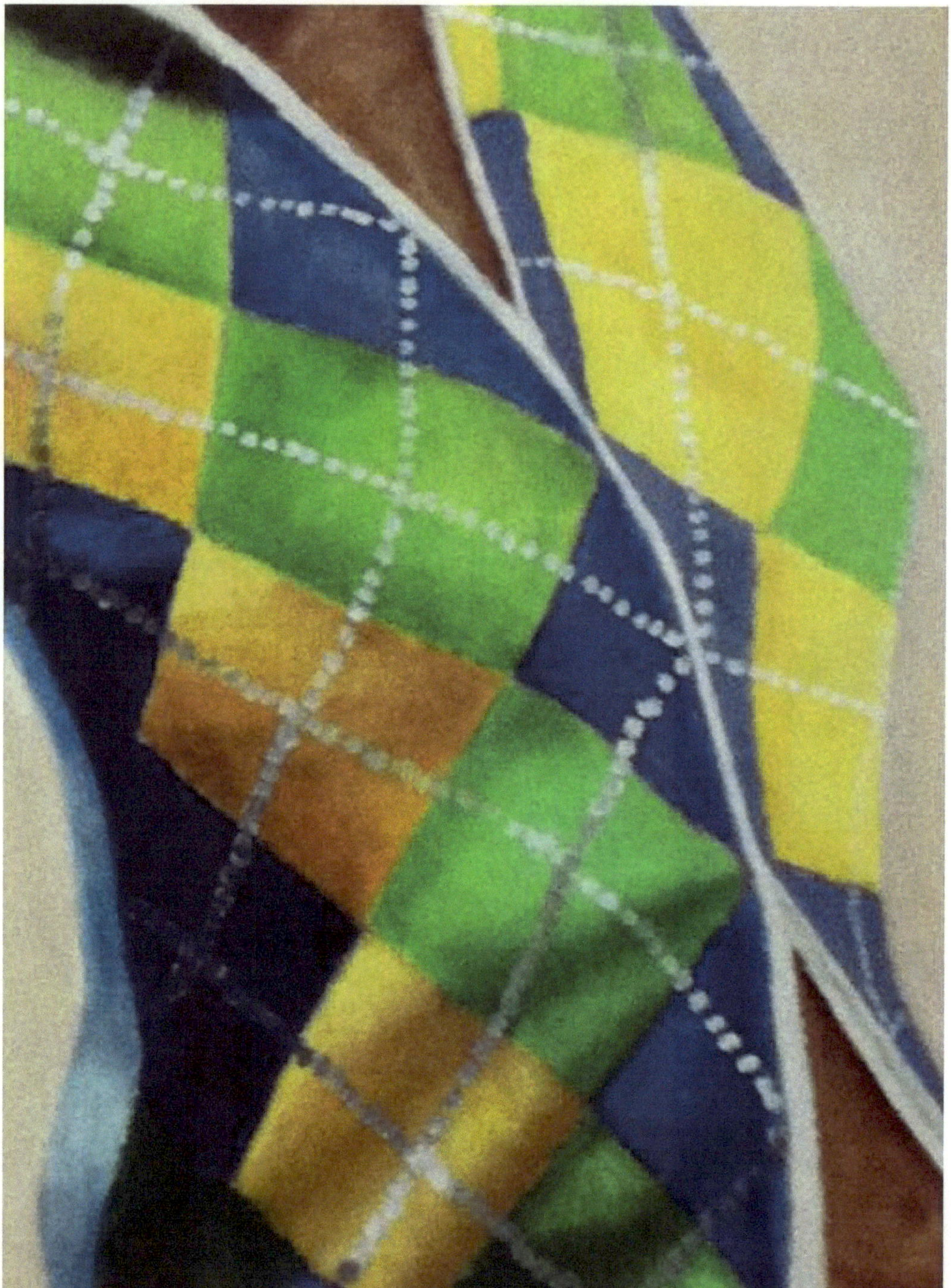

Oil on canvas 70 by 50 cm

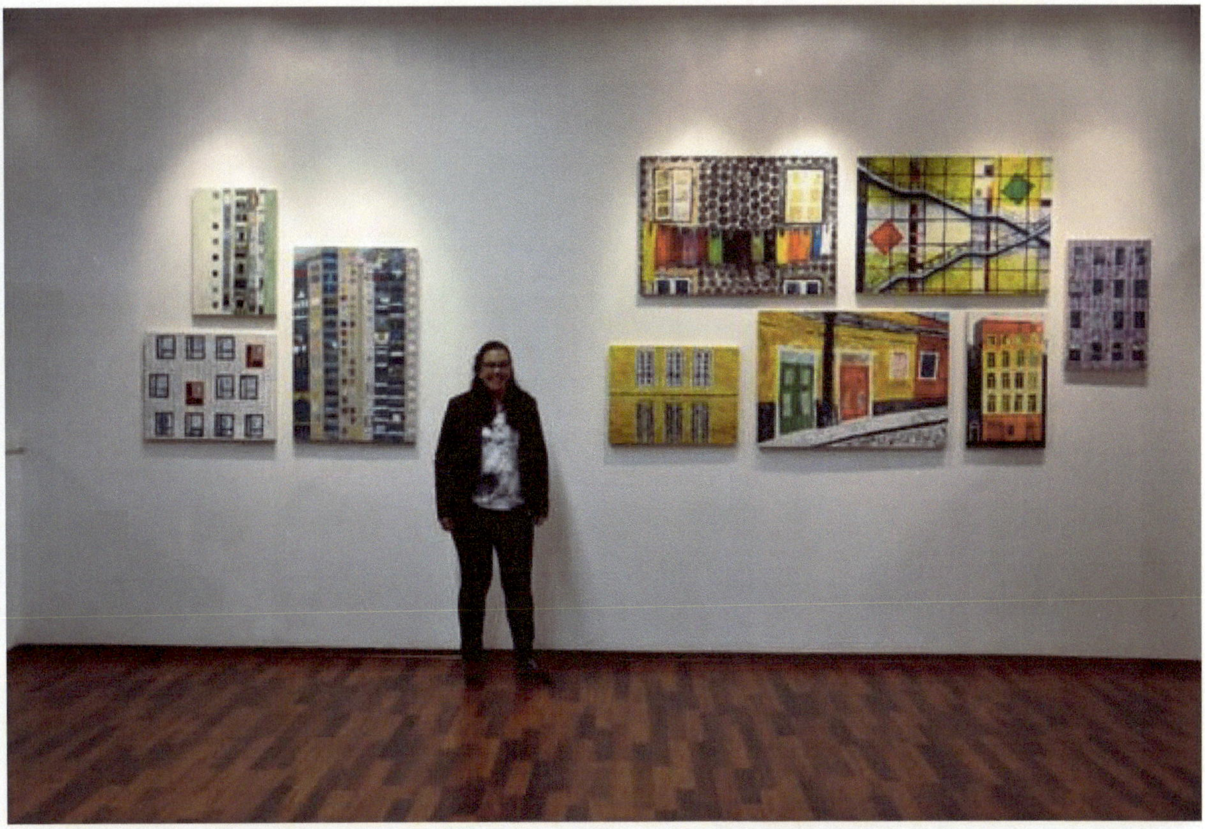

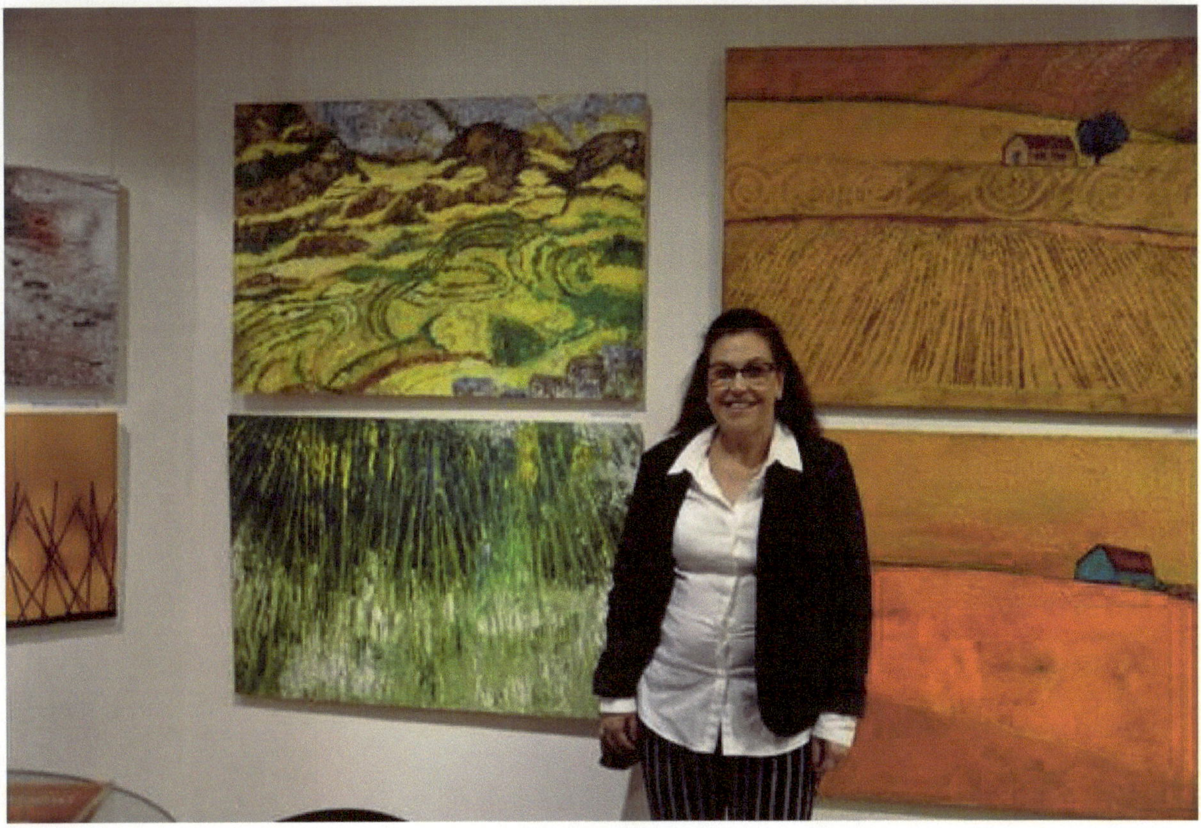

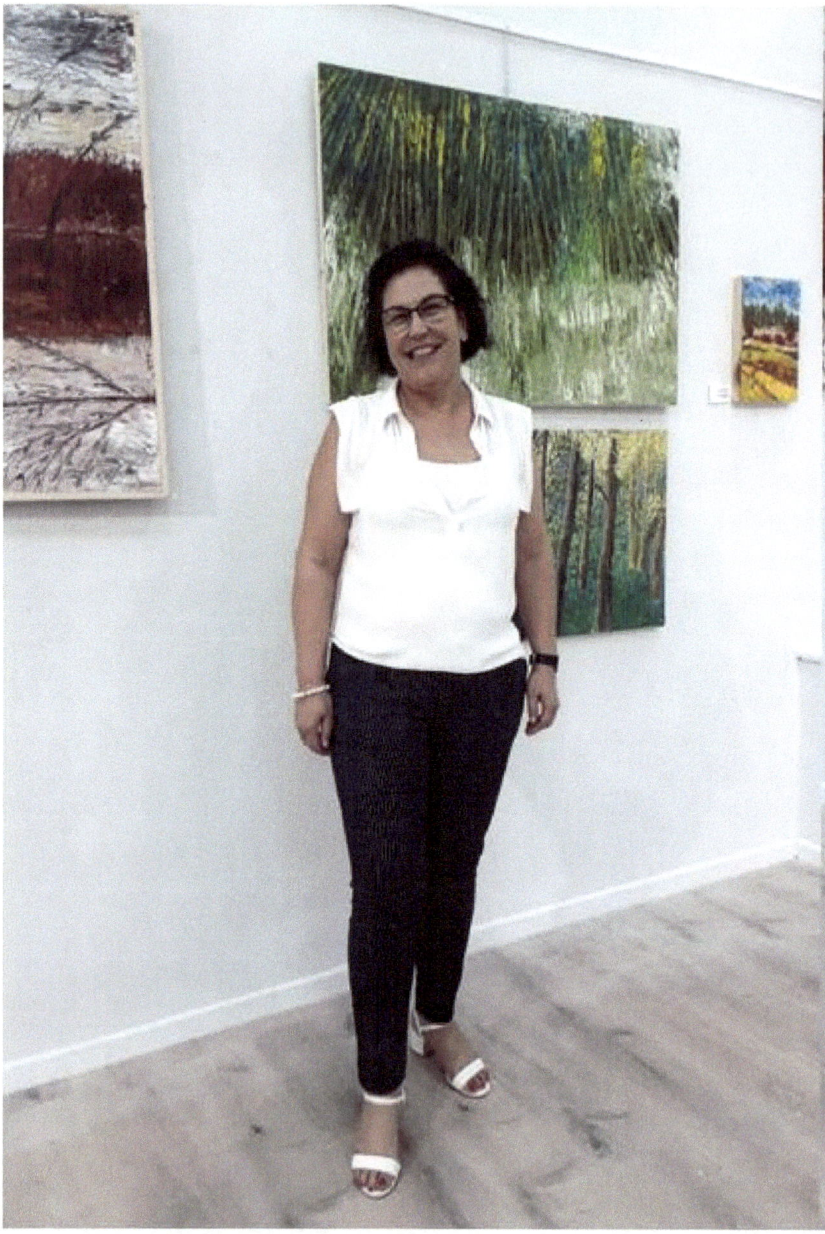

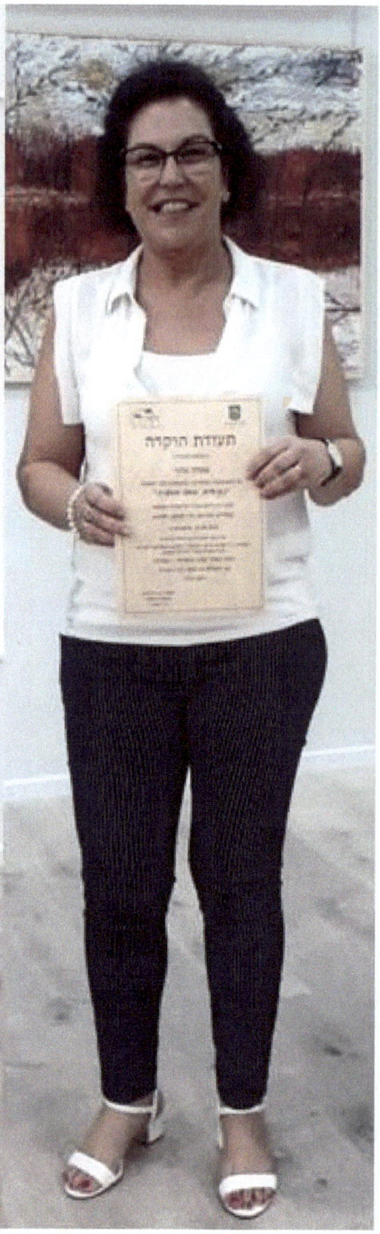